GW01605825

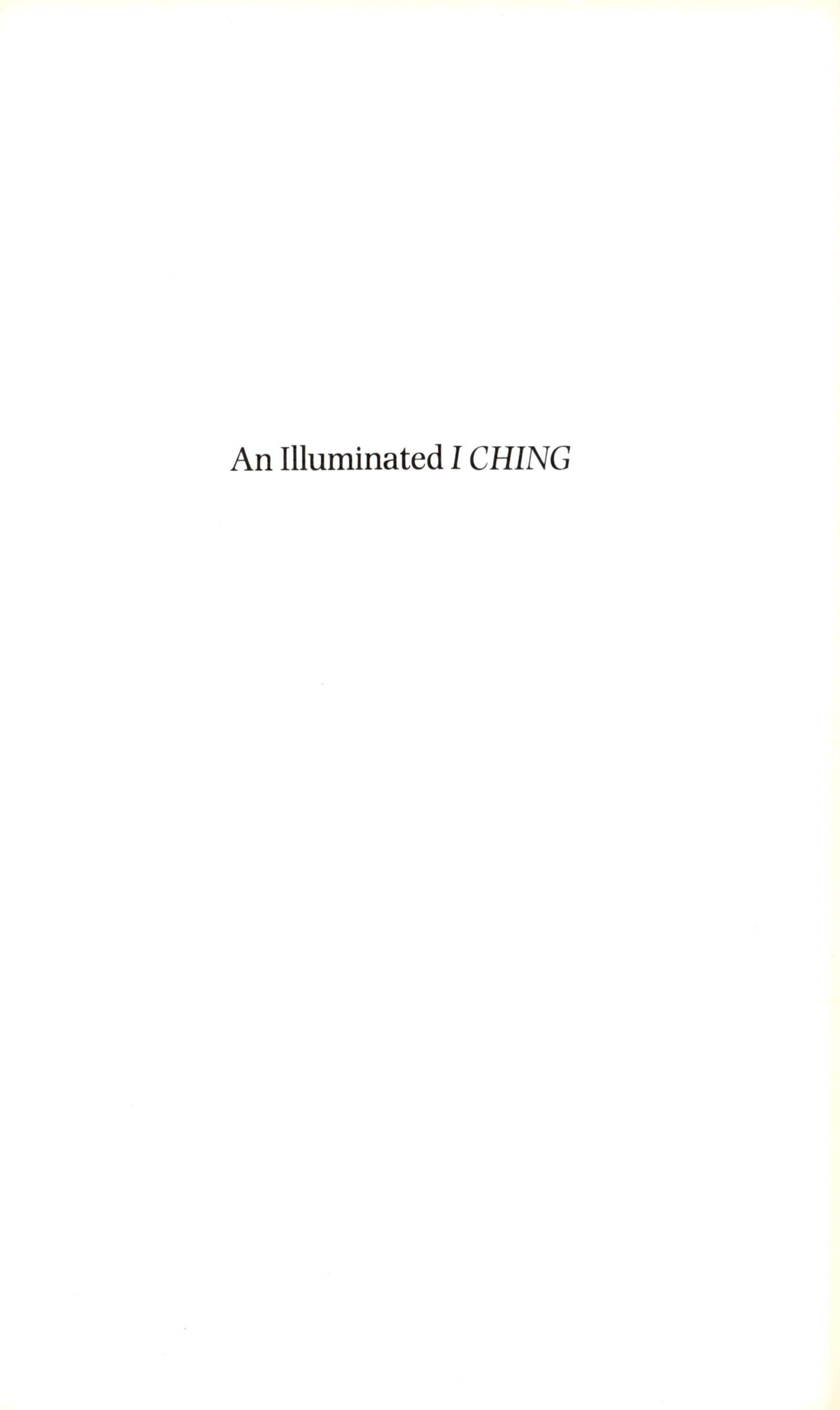

An Illuminated *I CHING*

An Illuminated
I CHING

By

Judy Fox
Karen Hughes
John Tampion

Neville Spearman
Suffolk

First published in Great Britain in 1982
by Neville Spearman Limited
The Priory Gate, Friars Street, Sudbury, Suffolk

ISBN 0 85435 025 X

Typeset in Photina and printed in Great Britain by the
White Crescent Press Ltd, Luton

Contents

Acknowledgements

1. To the *I Ching* and the Chinese civilization which created and preserved it over the centuries.
2. To all those who have laboured to translate, explain and understand the *I Ching*.
3. To John, Richard and Maureen, our respective husbands and wife, for supporting us in the preparation of this book and particularly to Maureen for typing the final version of the text.

How to Enter the *I Ching*

To use this book is simple. Take three similar, small, coins. Let each 'head' be equal to three and each 'tail' equal to two. Clasp the hands together and shake the coins gently in the chamber formed by the palms of the hands. At the same time think of the question on which you require guidance. If you have no particular question, the guidance will apply to your own situation at the present time. When you are satisfied with the amount of shaking you have given to the coins let them fall gently onto a flat surface. When they come to rest examine the upper surfaces and count up the total score. There are only four possibilities because the order in which the coins are examined does not matter.

This first throw will form the lowermost line of the six-line hexagram which you are about to construct. The hexagram is a symbolic representation of the wisdom of the *I Ching*.

If you have thrown the number 6 (three tails) or 8 (two heads and one tail) draw a broken line thus — —.

If you have thrown the number 7 (two tails and one head) or 9 (three heads) draw a solid line thus ——.

Although the lines are drawn in the same way there is an important distinction between the 6 and the 8 and also between the 7 and the 9. The 6 and 9 are called moving lines and should be marked for further attention when the hexagram is complete.

To complete the hexagram repeat the shaking and throwing of the coins with the same thoughts in mind and build up from the bottom (first) line to the top (sixth) line, noting any moving lines.

With the first hexagram complete the pattern is looked up in the list which follows. There are only sixty-four possible arrangements of the lines. At this stage no distinctions are made between moving lines and ordinary lines.

When the correct number of the hexagram has been found its guidance is available from the main text of this book, which is arranged in numerical order, according to the number given in the list. For this first hexagram read the Image and the Judgement and the text relating only to the moving lines which have been given. The guidance refers to the present situation. Where

The Hexagrams and their Numbers

Upper / Lower	Ch'ien	Tui	Li	Sun	Chen	K'an	Ken	K'un
Ch'ien	1	43	14	9	34	5	26	11
Tui	10	58	38	61	54	60	41	19
Li	13	49	30	37	55	63	22	36
Sun	44	28	50	57	32	48	18	46
Chen	25	17	21	42	51	3	27	24
K'an	6	47	64	59	40	29	4	7
Ken	33	31	56	53	62	39	52	15
K'un	12	45	35	20	16	8	23	2

the first hexagram contains 'moving' lines a second hexagram, referring to a possible future situation or outcome from the present, can be derived. Every 'moving' line is converted into its opposite type of line. No change is made in the other lines. This second hexagram can then be looked up in the list and text in the same way as the first hexagram. For the derived hexagram read the Image and the Judgement only.

In order to easily locate the hexagrams in the text a chart is given opposite in which the possible permutations of the eight trigrams are logically arranged. The actual arrangement of hexagrams used in the text is that normally used in other, fuller, versions of the *I Ching* and it has been retained for ease of cross-reference. The text order is attributed to King Wen (See later section on the History of the *I Ching*).

How to Understand the Illuminated *I Ching*

The *I Ching* is considered to be the oldest Book of Wisdom in the World that is still in current use. Its origins, in pre-Dynastic China, are obscure but its concepts were almost certainly in use for many centuries before they were written down and, inevitably, became more formalized. Unlike ancient religious books, however, there is no God in the *I Ching* to bring retribution to the wrong-doer nor salvation to the Believer. Instead, we find the distilled essence of Life Experience itself; the outcome of detailed and painstaking observations of Man and Nature, over the centuries.

It is an interesting reflection on modern life that the types of problems which the *I Ching* gives guidance on, seem to be recurring problems in every community of mankind and in any form of social organisation. Regardless of the time and place, problems occur in the relationships between individuals, between individuals and the community and between communities. The basic personality of Man has probably changed little in the millenia since the *I Ching* was first formulated. Even in the 1980s, when modern urban peoples have succeeded, in no small measure, in isolating themselves from the cycles of Nature, the sun still rises and sets; water still flows down to the sea and winter, spring, summer and autumn still inexorably follow one another. Despite the ever-accelerating progress of modern Science the vast majority of people still suffer problems to which there appears no simple solution, no rational basis for choice of action. Only in the most trivial circumstances can we see the causal relationship of an act on our part leading to a predetermined consequence. Any thought or act which we perform must influence the outside world and likewise, the outside world must influence us. The ripples of any event in the Universe must eventually reach each one of us. There is no simple answer as to when this will happen. Scientists can accurately predict the time it will take for half of the radioactive atoms in a gramme of material to 'decay' and lose their extra energy. They cannot predict which of the atoms will actually decay. Every atom is unique. Likewise, every person is unique and every second of time is unique.

The *I Ching* is based upon the concept of synchronicity. The unique situation which causes us to ask guidance of the *I Ching* meshes with the fall of the coins to produce a hexagram which synchronizes with our problem. If we asked the same question earlier or later we may well obtain a different hexagram with different guidance. An infinite series of the same enquiry would give us an infinite series of hexagrams, but this would be of no value to us. What concerns us is the best advice at this particular moment. A particular question should be asked only once in a day. Usually the advice we receive on the first occasion will remain relevant for days, weeks or even months. To keep asking the same question implies a lack of respect for the advice which the *I Ching* has given. Even the wisest person will feel insulted if his considered opinions are continually rejected as not appropriate to the problem in hand. When we have the best advice there is no need to seek further viewpoints but merely to act upon it. Without doubt our actions, consciously and unconsciously, will affect the future in ways which we cannot imagine – a thesis strongly supported by Al Koran and his experiences (1972).

In any situation there is a multitude of possible courses of action. The route which the *I Ching* suggests is that to be followed by the wise person. This is also the course of action which is in tune with the Laws of Nature, the unavoidable morality of the Universe. In the original text and in the illuminated symbolism used in the present version the emphasis is often upon the changing seasons. There is no point in planting a summer seed in winter – it cannot withstand the cold so it cannot grow and flourish. There are sympathetic times for all things. We have the free will to plant our 'seeds' at the wrong time of the year but our free choice is doomed to failure if we go too far against natural laws. How we act on the advice of the *I Ching* depends ultimately on ourselves. At certain times action is called for, at others no progress can be made and we must conserve our resources or make alternative plans.

Any problem put to the *I Ching* must be phrased in such a way that the meaning of the answer is clear. We cannot ask a double either/or question since we will not be able to decide which of the two questions is being answered. The request must be direct so that the answer will also be direct. Exactly how we act upon the advice is something that we must, in the end, decide. If the answer seems obscure there is obviously a need to discuss it with others. This might be a professional who specializes in interpreting the *I Ching* in the context of other peoples' problems or, more often, one's closest relative or friend. If nobody is available ponder the answer for twenty-four hours. If it is still not clear try again, perhaps with a rephrased question.

What if you cannot formulate a particular question or merely wish to know the general situation and prospects? In this case one approaches the *I Ching* as a wise friend. Concentrate merely on the shaking of the coins rather than a specific question. The hexagram will then be generally applicable to you and should be interpreted accordingly.

Most serious students of the *I Ching* soon begin to keep their own log-book or diary of questions, situations, answers and interpretations. This can be further annotated with events as they subsequently unfold. Only in this way will the true significance of the *I Ching* be discovered.

The *I Ching* is both a spiritual and a materialistic book, teaching the development of inner strength of character and its outward expression in actual deeds. The present *Illuminated I Ching* is constructed on a similar dualistic approach. The very abbreviated version of the text which we give is essentially materialistic in the advice it gives for dealing with problems. Virtually all the symbolism of the original text has been removed but the central concepts retained in a form as close as possible to the original. The illuminated hexagrams and illustrations express the more spiritual and mystical aspects. In no way should they be dismissed as mere ornamentation. Before reading the text of any hexagram the reader may find it helpful to first look at the illumination. After reading the text it could then be contemplated again, together with any illustration which is provided. Drawings and words complement one another.

A proper consideration of the meaning and symbolism of the lines which make up the hexagram would fill many books and has, indeed, already done so. In this text we have done no more than pick out the two trigrams – the upper and lower 'outer' trigrams – which make up each hexagram. There are also 'inner' trigrams which comprise lines 2, 3, 4 and 3, 4, 5 respecively. In addition, each individual line has particular meaning, both as picked out by the 'moving' lines and also as represented by the particular line positions, which represent different family and social relationships.

The eight possible trigrams each have an impressive list of attributes associated with them. Again, we have only taken the very first of these, derived mostly from observation of the changing forces of nature. This has been included in both the text and the illuminations. For the convenience of the reader these are summarized on page 14.

Although some versions of the *I Ching* make much use of the yang/yin terminology we have deliberately not done so. These words and their symbolism are almost certainly later additions to the original interpretations of the lines. We do not object to their use but merely believe that they form a complication which should be added later by the readers themselves.

The drawings in this book all follow the same format. The circle, denoting heaven is enclosed by the square, denoting earth, reflecting the inevitable integration of these two concepts to the life of man. The background patterns are reminders of the 'elements' associated with the eight trigrams, as given above. The corners, formed of both straight and curved lines are reminders of some of the aspects of change found in nature. Thus the cycles of the seasons, of water,. of growth, death and regeneration and of the motions of the heavenly bodies are all evident. Much of the wisdom of the *I Ching* derives from the philosophical and scientific observation of the natural laws and phenomena of the Universe. In Nature there is a continual change, yet with an underlying pattern which recurs on a time-scale commensurate with its inherent principles. In the study of human nature, too, there would appear to be nothing new in the interactions between people, both as individuals and as units of society. In the separate illustrations which accompany some hexagrams an attempt has been made to emphasize certain aspects of the symbolism mentioned in the original text. Where this symbolism is not easily apparent from our abbreviated text we recommend an even closer contemplation of the illustration. The purpose of all the drawings is, of course, to encourage such contemplation both of oneself, one's position among family, friends and society, and one's place in the natural world. Only from such considerations can the meaning of life be explored.

For those new to such an approach the following brief comments may be of help.

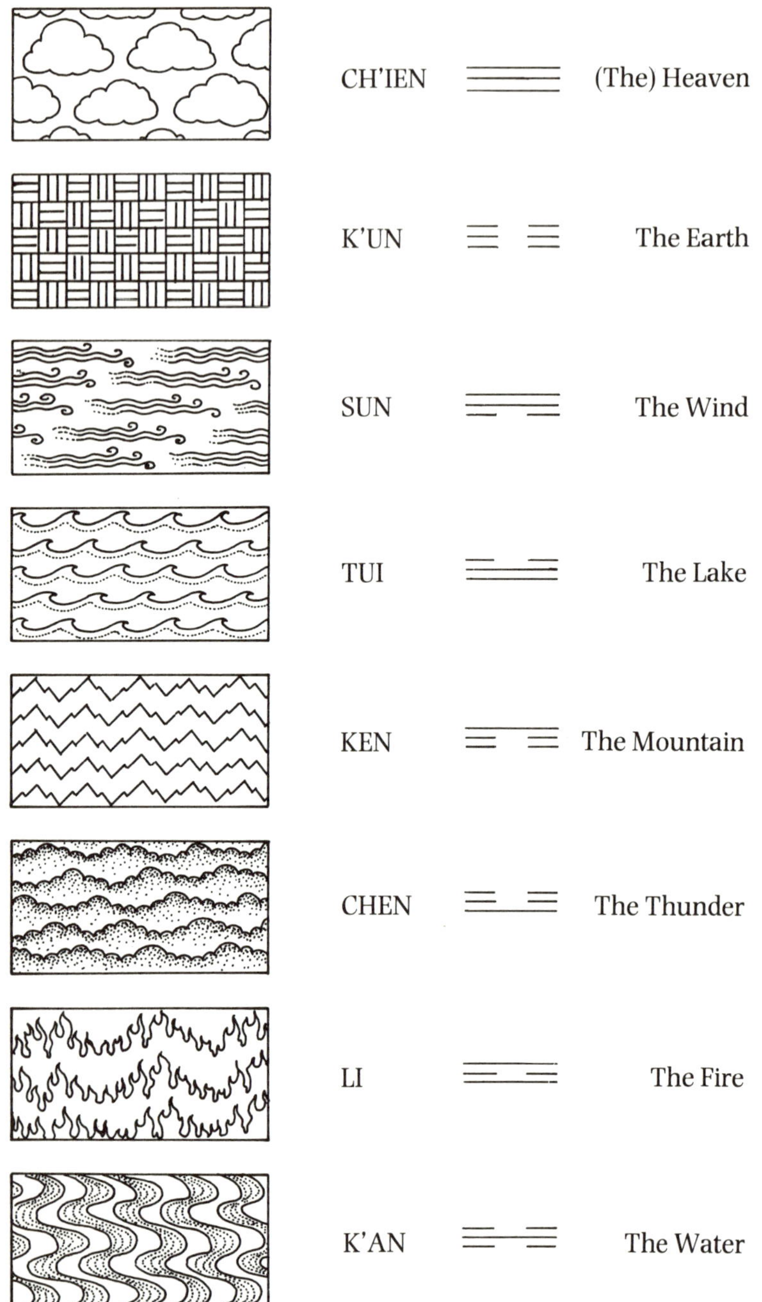
CH'IEN (The) Heaven
K'UN The Earth
SUN The Wind
TUI The Lake
KEN The Mountain
CHEN The Thunder
LI The Fire
K'AN The Water

Dragon:
A non-materialistic creature of the air and heavens, not to be confused with the dragons of the middle and later ages in Europe. Its attributes cover creativity, imagination and affairs of the spirit.

Mare:
An obviously earthly creature, always aware of its surrounding, always observant of the changes around it, both the dangers and the opportunities. Although bound to the earth it still has, at speed, the freedom of it.

Water:
A substance which never loses its own identity, yet can take on the external form of anything it finds itself in. It proceeds on its way regardless of all danger. Steep precipices, deep ravines, dark underground caverns and open lakes all contain it, but in a manner which is both temporary and permanent. It is responsive to the other elements yet never truly lost. In gentleness it brings life and fertility to all things but in anger it has an awesome power, sweeping aside Man's puny efforts.

Seasons:
The cycles of birth, growth, maturity, senescence and decay apply to all things on the earth. Plants, animals, humans and their families and societies travel the same road. From the end of one cycle another begins; nothing material can last forever. Daily, monthly, yearly, by tens, sixties, hundreds, thousands or millions, time always moves onwards, yet also recycles, from the movements of the earth, moon, planets, solar system, Universe and Cosmos. A truly inexhaustible source of imagery, symbolism and knowledge.

A word here on the sexuality of the *I Ching* is appropriate. When originally put into written form, and indeed until comparatively recently, the relationship between the roles of men and women in the family and society has been markedly polarized. Much of the original *I Ching* text reflects this. We have been at pains to remove those aspects which we consider to be at odds with the present place of women in both the home and society. It is, perhaps, worth mentioning that at one stage it was our intention to attempt a redress of this imbalance by producing a specifically woman's *I Ching*. Relatively little thought, however, is needed to see that this would merely serve to re-emphasize the divisions between male and female. Wherever the male gender is used in our version of the text this is used entirely for the purpose of simplifying the expression of complex ideas. The reader should substitute the appropriate sex, as relevant to the problem at hand. This is not to say that male and female (or yang and yin) are equivalent concepts in themselves. As the *I Ching* itself continuously re-emphasizes, they are complementary concepts in which one has to appreciate the nature of both to achieve understanding.

This small book which your are currently reading is only the very edge of the *I Ching*. When you have passed through the gateway it offers and want a deeper appreciation, seek out the full text, then the commentaries on it and finally the limitless ramifications and applications of it which have been developed over the centuries. The present authors will be happy if they have helped the reader to take a first step in that direction, away from indecision and being a victim of circumstances and towards a position of being able to see things and people in the correct perspective and relationship to one another. The Way is not easy, for in the World of the *I Ching* we cannot escape our problems. We must shoulder our burdens and act in accord with our responsibilities. Only then can we come to terms with Life and all it brings. There is no short cut, no drug, no ritual, no 'five-minutes-a-day' method to find the True Way. Life is a Total Experience and Reality arises from Within.

The History of the *I Ching*

Like all books of extremely ancient origin the exact way in which the *I Ching* was first conceived is not known to us. In fact, there are few, if any, books still in use today which can be traced back as far as the *I Ching*. In the English-speaking world the Old Testament must be the nearest equivalent. A major difference does arise, however, because the *I Ching* is not a religious book in which the existence of and belief in a particular form of Supreme Being must be accepted. The *I Ching* is compatible with every religion and with no religious conviction at all. It is compatible also with any form of political organization because it gives individual guidance. True, there are and always have been some systems in which the advice of the *I Ching* has fallen upon deaf ears. The ears, however, are always those of individuals because public morality arises from individual morality. There is no place for hypocrisy when the *I Ching* is studied. The persecuted prisoner, the lowliest slave, can be the superior person – the immoral strongman and the selfish weakling must, inevitably, be inferior.

Regrettably, our knowledge of ancient Chinese culture is very sketchy. Certainly it is one of the oldest civilizations. Only in recent times have archaeologists begun to unravel the splendours of the Chinese past. Unlike the blatant symbols of the long and defunct Dynasties of Ancient Egypt those of China, like the *I Ching*'s wisdom itself, must be painstakingly sought out. The direct graphology of the lines – scratches and the gaps between them, is the simplest possible type of human non-verbal communication. It must have arisen prior to any other form of non-mental information storage and exchange. According to tradition the legendary Fu Hsi first created the trigrams and combined them into hexagrams some 5,000 years ago. He is also credited with the creation of the first Chinese Civilization. In other words, he provided the guidance which enabled individuals to work together and create civilization. Among many others, the Yellow Emperor (Huang Ti) is particularly credited with promoting the *I Ching* around 4,400 years ago. A feature which has led to the survival of the *I Ching* is the fact that, being entirely neutral in its stance with authority (although certainly decisive about right and wrong actions) it has not been subjected to repeated official 're-interpretation'. This regrettably, was the fate of that other ancient text, the Shu Ching which has an historical aspect of chronicling the reigns and actions of emperors and kings.

In the absence of writing materials, the basic symbols were recorded by carrying readily available material, such as bones and shells. Tortoiseshell had a particular significance in ancient China and was often also used for divination. The pattern of cracks which develop when it is heated were interpreted, rather like the more mundane tea-leaves of certain fortune-tellers. The Chinese characters which represent the hexagrams are also often attributed to Fu Hsi. Certainly they appear, from available archaeological evidence, to have first arisen in the north-west of China. This may, naturally enough, date from the origin of Chinese writing itself, some 4,000 years ago. The first 'books' appear to have been made of bamboo strips on which the characters could be burnt to give a permanent record. Since these books appear to have been tied together and rolled up into bundles the natural form of writing would be with the lines running vertically, from top to bottom of the strips. Assuming a preponderance of right-handed scribes, the text would also naturally flow from the right to the left. There is no other simple way of holding a scroll to write on it without the use of a table or other elaborate equipment as a support. The origin of writing in other civilizations likewise bears a significant relationship to the properties of the available writing materials. At the time of its first writing down the *I Ching* can only have consisted of very abbreviated texts associated with the hexagrams – a starting point for individual interpretation and extrapolation.

The form in which the central core of the *I Ching* now exists is attributed to King Wen and the Duke of Chou. In accord with our previous comments it is interesting to note that Wen carried out his work on the *I Ching* as a prisoner of the last emperor of the Shang (Yin) dynasty. He explained the Images and the Judgements at that time, just over 3,000 years ago. His son Wu, now known as the Duke of Chou, overthrew the Shang and started the Chou dynasty. He posthumously elevated his father to the title of King and continued his work on the *I Ching* by adding explanations for the moving lines. Thus it is that the wording and imagery of straight translations of the *I Ching* is appropriate to the situation in China some 3,000 years ago and hence, inevitably, cryptic in the present age.

Confucius, some 2,600 years ago, added important commentaries to the *I Ching*, which have remained with it to this day. At almost the same time Lao Tze wrote his *Tao Te Ching*, which drew upon the *I Ching* for some of its inspiration. This work forms an important study point for the religion of Taoism – a subject of life-time studies in its own right. For nearly 300 years after the time of Confucius there was considerable turmoil in China (the Warring States period) and many reinterpretations and comments on the *I Ching* were set down. From this chaos, in 213 BC, came the orders of the Emperor Chin to put a stop to this melting-pot of ideas by burning all books which did not conform to his ideals. The basic *I Ching* was allowed to remain but among those parts which were destroyed were the commentaries of Confucius. Like so many grandiose schemes to change the world this one also failed because certain people beyond the reach of the law were able to retain their books. These survived into the Han dynasty (206 BC) and with several of Confucius's other works became the foundation of education for administrators over the subsequent centuries. These 'set books' were the reading matter for the examination system of those times. From this firm basis the study of the *I Ching* has continued, albeit with variable effort and quality, up to the present day. Sometimes its guidance has been frowned upon by those in authority. At other times they have lent it their support.

There can be no doubt that the *I Ching* would not have survived had it not contained something of supreme value. We are as much in need of its guidance, based upon universal, if self-evident truths (the true Laws of Nature) as were the illiterate people of 5,000 years ago. Human nature has not changed in that period. True, the choices have become more complex, but our intuitive understanding of what is right remains unaltered. It is this very essence that we have attempted here, in our small book, to crystallize and offer to the reader. Because of our present mastery of certain facets of the world about us, it is easier now, than ever before, to follow paths of life which are not in sympathy with the Laws of Nature. Such paths must, inevitably, lead to obstructions. The *I Ching* is not about dull restrictions on free-will or some ethic imposed from outside. It is about living life to its full, being creative, directing our own course and, hence that of others who come into contact with us, towards supreme fulfilment. So many people have not yet found the door within themselves which opens to the Universe. Once unlocked, the path of the *I Ching* is clear.

The Philosophy of the *I Ching*

Many millions of words have been written concerning the philosophical aspects of the *I Ching*. The original version of this part of our book was almost complete when, by a chance event, a totally new light was shed upon its significance. Before we reach that point, however, the more frequently quoted ideas must first be summarized.

The title *I Ching* is generally translated as: *The Book of Changes*. It is this aspect of change which is fundamental to the *I Ching*, coupled with the concept of opposite, but complementary states. Everywhere we look in both the material and spiritual world we find this concept of opposites. Good and Evil; God and the Devil; Man and Woman; Positive and Negative. But each concept only has meaning in terms of its complementary opposite. In the initial imagery of the *I Ching* we have the simplistic representation of the two states as solid or broken lines. At a later date this becomes expressed more clearly by the symbolism of Yin and Yang (with each arising from the other), which became incorporated into, or may indeed have arisen from, the *I Ching*. In the philosophy of the *I Ching* nothing is ever static, everything is in motion. Just as in life, nothing can ever remain the same. Perhaps this is the true message – teaching the reader to be humble before the laws of Nature. If one has reached the apogee in any matter, the progress can only be downwards. At the nadir progress can only be upwards. Time does not leave anything behind.

The origin of the nature symbolism of the *I Ching* must obviously have been the natural world itself, external to the thoughtful observer. At the same time, however, the observer cannot escape from being part of Nature. The laws which direct Nature likewise direct the life of mankind. What more reasonable concept than that by studying the cycles of nature we can understand our own existence. But blind fatalism is not part of the *I Ching*. Man, uniquely amongst the living organisms of the Earth, can foresee, if he has the wisdom, the outcome of his own actions. Careful observation of nature reveals certain rules. Water flows downwards. The tension before a storm is dissipated by the thunder and lightning, leaving everything refreshed.

The inevitable sequel to observing natural events is to observe the actions of Man. The levels of observation spread like the ripples on a pond. If we start with a single person the influence spreads out through family relationships to friends and working colleagues and beyond that person's own knowledge of his influence to encompass the whole world. The stumbling block which restricts the development of awareness by the western mind is the concept of causality. Because it has been indoctrinated into us from our earliest days it is extremely difficult to set aside the belief that every event has some immediate cause, that every action has some inevitable outcome. When two events occur, for which our limited horizons can find no simple causal relationship, we put this down to 'chance' or 'coincidence'. Many volumes have been filled with mathematical and philosophical discussions of the meaning of chance. Indeed we have been led to believe that the probability of an event happening, as calculated by the most elaborate statistical techniques, actually means something.

A classical example of this dilemma, as quoted a few pages ago, is our view of the disintegration of a radioactive substance. It is possible to calculate very accurately how long it will take for half the atoms of a radioisotope sample to decay away. It is impossible, however, to say how long any particular atom will exist before it decays. It may disintegrate at the moment of our observation or it may remain intact for thousands of years. In the same way, in our own daily lives, events may be very probable and yet never happen or very unlikely and yet happen in the next minute. The problem in our daily lives is that we often cannot decide what course of action to adopt. Nor can we comprehend the 'significant coincidence' when two totally (as far as we can tell) unrelated events occur together. This idea has been investigated by many scholars and much has been written about it. We are on the fringe also of such paranormal phenomena as ESP.

The *I Ching* is based, quite simply, on the idea of 'significant coincidence' or, as it is more usually described, the principle of synchronicity. Carl Jung in his masterful foreword to the Wilhelm translation of the *I Ching* discusses this point. Briefly, the throw of the coins, or the manipulation of the yarrow stalks in the traditional Chinese method, forms a synchronous event with our search for guidance from the *I Ching*. The meaning of this coincidence we can obtain from the text of the *I Ching*. But the *I Ching* is not a character study of the enquirer nor an unalterable prediction of the future. Instead, it offers advice as to how we can best conduct ourselves in the present circumstance and hence achieve an accord with the inevitable forces of nature. Its advice, therefore, is built upon careful observation of the human situations over thousands of years. The expressions and human imagery used in the Chinese version of the *I Ching* are based upon the intuitive understanding of its largely unknown original authors, amplified over the centuries by the thoughts of a few intellectual giants, as noted in the previous section. Up to the present version, people in the Western world have been prepared simply to treat it as an academic work, to be translated most carefully and painstakingly, and reproduced with unchanged Chinese imagery. Regretfully, this provides a serious block to the more general acceptance of the present-day value of the *I Ching*, except for the intellectual few. As previously explained the purpose of our version is to convey the intuitive content of the *I Ching* without the impediment of minutiae. The more literal translations should be sought out when our small text has been understood. We seek only to open the gate.

What of this totally new light on the *I Ching*? It was, as might be anticipated, an example of synchronicity. The chance finding of a book on a library shelf. The clarity of the explanation stems directly from David Foster's fascinating book *The Intelligent Universe*. If we may be forgiven for such a brief resumé of his work, the central concept is that there is a distinct analogy, if not exact equivalence, between the functioning of an electronic computer and the functioning of the Universe. To those who do not understand the computer we must offer a word of instruction. To carry out computing (data processing) we require certain levels of relationship which cannot be interchanged. At the lowest we have the actual data itself. This is acted upon by a computer program (software) which carries out certain previously defined actions. The program was created by the programmer. The programmer made up this particular program to achieve certain previously defined specific Aims. These specific Aims were defined to achieve an overall master plan (harmony) for the whole enterprise. It can be seen that this relationship is entirely one-way. The data can never know the program nor influence it. In the world of human experience we find those who behave like data, moved willy-nilly by the actions of others, withdrawing from reality, because it seems too harsh. Everywhere we see both the ancient and the latest modern aids used to ensure that the majority of people stay at this lowest state.

Those who can fulfil themselves, fit themselves into the proper pattern of the Universe, are those who can understand the program. A fortunate few appear able to write their own program. For the majority we need to use a ready-made one. Quite simply, the *I Ching* is a program for living, developed over the centuries to be of Universal application. This relationship to the electronic computer can be taken a stage further. Our electronic computers operate on the binary code principle. The units in a computer can exist in only two states and the program switches them from one to another. Does not the *I Ching* work on exactly the same principle?

With the guidance of the *I Ching* we can find a way forward. Darkness can be turned into Light. Only the receptive soul, however, can find within itself a true path to follow, leading wheresoever it may. Those who do not seek a full knowledge of themselves cannot expect to find an harmonious route through the life experience.

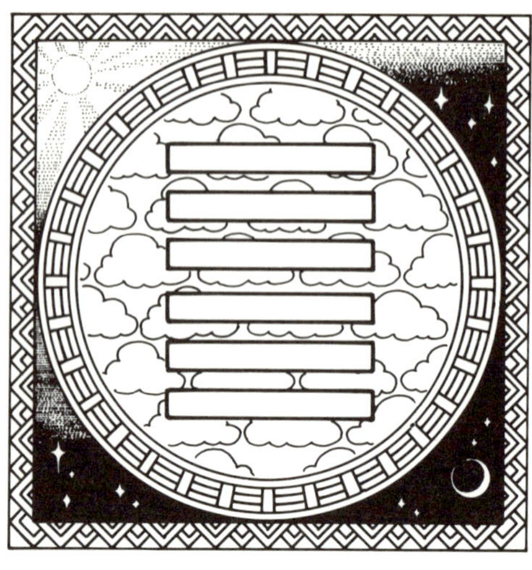

1. CH'IEN
Productive Action

Ch'ien over Ch'ien
Heaven over Heaven

The Image
The universe is moved by a power which cycles endlessly from day to day. Such greatness endures for all time. As in heaven, so on earth.

The Judgement
To achieve absolute success one's creative forces must be continuously applied.

Progress towards the ultimate in life can only be made along the path which accords with the Laws of the Universe. We may all have great ideas but it is the application of a creative force which makes them a reality. If the ideas do not conform to the true nature of things, or the path is a devious one, greatness cannot be achieved. Success will only be gained by ensuring that one's actions are in harmony with the Universe.

The Lines

9 in the 1st
When the outside world is ready great ideas will be accepted. In the meantime they cannot be forced onto others, but must be kept undiminished.

9 in the 2nd
When we discern a person of great worth, even though they have not yet achieved greatness, it will be of benefit to follow their advice.

9 in the 3rd
A door to achievement is opening but to follow the path requires unswaying integrity. Ambition and undeserved praise can lead away from what is right.

9 in the 4th
The choice must be made between the path of public acclaim and the path of obscurity and introspection. Each person must make their own choice.

9 in the 5th
Each to his own. If we would seek greatness we must follow great men.

9 in the 6th
Beware the dangers of excess. Do not put yourself above the rest of humanity.

9 in all places
Strength and humility unite. Greatness comes from the gentle application of what is correct. The end does not justify the means.

2. K'UN
Receptivity

K'un over K'un
Earth over Earth

The Image
The planet Earth endures and carries with it both good and evil. The great person, with breadth of character, can sustain the good and endure the evil.

The Judgement
The wise person will follow good advice and continue along the correct path in all that is done.

Help is needed to express all one's potential to its full extent but time must be set aside to prepare a course of action that will be successful. There must be leaders and followers who complement one another. In the world of Nature sickness and health, prey and predator exist together. If fate is accepted, then the best course of action can be chosen and progress made.

The Lines

6 in the 1st
Action must be taken at the first signs of disruption or decay, otherwise disaster will follow as ice-bound winter follows brief autumn frosts.

6 in the 2nd
The great person's achievements grow one from another and all his actions are clearly visible. The Forces of Nature create change. Each creature plays a part in this.

6 in the 3rd
Do not draw attention to your actions to receive praise but continue quietly with the work for its future completion.

6 in the 4th
The time is not yet ripe for action. Mingle with the crowd or withdraw to solitude. In dangerous times the wise person must remain silent to prevent the creation of wrong impressions which may cause jealousy or misplaced acclaim.

6 in the 5th
The great person, when working in a subordinate position, must show complete discretion. Excellence should only show in the quality of the work.

6 in the 6th
To attempt to rule instead of serve will bring disaster to all. Everybody will suffer injury.

6 in all places
The excellence of proper actions will endure. They will neither magnify nor diminish.

3. CHUN
Initial Adversity

K'an over Chen
Water over Thunder

The Image
Thunder and dark clouds may appear chaotic but after the storm order will return. The wise man progresses by sorting and combining the good aspects. A germinating seed may find it difficult to push its way out of the ground.

The Judgement
At the birth of any great new activity there is always difficulty and danger. The great person toils and provides guidance, but he must have helpers. New courses of action should not be rushed into.

The Lines
9 in the 1st
If a difficulty is found at the start the objectives must be held in mind but the pathway replanned. Associates must not be domineered, but instead should be quietly convinced of the value of a project.

6 in the 2nd
When we are beset with difficulties we should not accept help from an unexpected quarter which places us under an obligation. After a time, which may be very long, success will arrive.

6 in the 3rd
Without guidance difficulties cannot be overcome. To push on blindly leads to failure. Take advice, if necessary change your plans.

6 in the 4th
When we must act, but lack the ability, we should not be too proud to accept help. The true helper can take us forward.

9 in the 5th
When the resolution of a problem is difficult and disrupted by people creating a misunderstanding, we must move forward quietly and slowly. To attempt a great leap will bring failure.

6 in the 6th
For some persons, the initial difficulties may be too great and a good scheme abandoned as impossible. This is a sad event.

4. MENG
Youthful Immaturity

Ken over K'an
Mountain over Water

The Image
The water from a spring flows on steadily, filling up all depressions but never stagnating. The wise person is thorough in all he does, no points are missed.

The Judgement
It is sensible that those who are inexperienced seek advice from the wise, but the wise man does not offer his council unsolicited. Wisdom is not achieved by constantly leaning on the strength of a great person. Follow the path one step at a time, not questioning good advice.

The Lines
6 in the 1st
To be successful in life requires discipline, but this should not become mere ritual which stifles initiative.

9 in the 2nd
The responsible person will tolerate the weakness and folly of others but, safe in his own inner strength, will still be able to achieve success.

6 in the 3rd
Only a weak person throws away his individuality to imitate another. No wise person will accept such foolish adoration.

6 in the 4th
When meeting a fool, who is wrapped up in his own empty thoughts, the wise person has no alternative but to let him learn from his own stupidity.

6 in the 5th
If we would learn from the wise, we should not pretend to be cleverer than we are.

9 in the 6th
Punishment should not be meted out in anger. It must fulfil the purpose of preventing unreasonable excesses by others.

5. HSU
Patience

K'an over Ch'ien
Water over Heaven

The Image
When clouds form in the skies we know that rain will follow but we must not wait for it. Nothing will be achieved by attempting to interfere with the future before the time is ripe. Patience is needed.

The Judgement
To be successful we must wait resolutely till the time is right, persevering along the correct pathway till the end is achieved. This is not blind fatalism, but instead reflects an ability to see things as they are and hence find the way to fulfilment. In this manner, when the opportunity comes, we shall be ready to make the right decision.

The Lines
9 in the 1st
Dangers are as yet only on the horizon. We must not waste our resources prematurely but must continue normally, for the present.

9 in the 2nd
The time of dangerous decisions is coming closer, but we must hold steadfastly to what is right. Injured pride must be endured quietly.

9 in the 3rd
It is not wise to make a premature attempt at overcoming the problem. When we act, our resources must be sufficient to carry us to the end.

6 in the 4th
We are now at the moment of danger but have no room to manoeuvre. Events must take their own course.

9 in the 5th
There are moments, even in dangerous times, when we must be able to relax and prepare for further action. The end is not lost to sight, our reserves are strengthened.

6 in the 6th
The danger is with us and we can see no way out. Unexpected visitors or events arrive, but we must treat them with thoughtful respect. Good fortune often comes via an unexpected route.

6. SUNG
Disagreement

Ch'ien over K'an
Heaven over Water

The Image
Heaven arises above but water must flow downwards. Conflicts can be avoided if careful thought is given, at the beginning, to define relationships.

The Judgement
Opposition to a path of action which one knows to be right should be met half-way. In this way enmity is not carried beyond the goal. An external, impartial, authority may be needed to judge the issues. If there is disagreement do not attempt any great projects.

The Lines

6 in the 1st
If a conflict is developing and the opponent is stronger do not proceed. In the end, it will be for the better.

9 in the 2nd
There is no dishonour in withdrawing from an unequal struggle. Others will also be hurt.

6 in the 3rd
Only what we have achieved by our own worth is permanently ours. The task should be the reward and not the praise for doing it.

9 in the 4th
A discontented person, who seeks conflict with another, can never be happy with himself, even if he wins. Accepting one's fate will bring harmony to life.

9 in the 5th
An independent arbitrator can be confidently expected to give the right answer.

9 in the 6th
If a conflict is taken to its ultimate limits the triumph will be short-lived, for someone else will win next time, and the conflict will never be resolved.

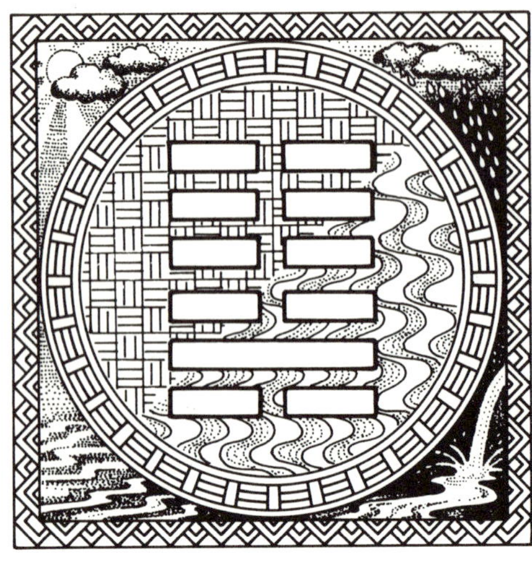

7. SHIH

Acting together

K'un over K'an
Earth over Water

The Image

Water is stored invisible in the earth, sheltered from evaporation, but available when required. In the same way the strength of any organisation, the people themselves, resides quietly inside. When properly cared for, their support makes the organisation impregnable. This, for example, is how any army should be.

The Judgement

A disorientated group of people must have a leader to direct their efforts to the tasks before them. Everybody must know and accept the aims and be convinced of the integrity of their leader. Drastic action, however, should only be undertaken, like war, as a last resort and when victory comes, this must not be an excuse for unjust vengeance.

The Lines

6 in the 1st
At the start of any project the objectives must be clear and reasonable and the personnel well-organised, otherwise failure is inevitable.

9 in the 2nd
A leader must be with his people during both good and bad fortune. When success is achieved and the leader is honoured, so are his people.

6 in the 3rd
When the correct person is not allowed to take charge, or a usurper intervenes for the leadership of an enterprise, misfortune must follow.

6 in the 4th
When the odds are overwhelming against one it is foolish to struggle on. Draw back sensibly to avoid defeat.

6 in the 5th
When the time for action has arrived, to defend something from an enemy, it must be carried out justly, under proper leadership. Mob rule will bring misfortune.

6 in the 6th
At the end of a struggle those involved should be rewarded, each according to his worth. Bestowing greater honour or gifts on someone unworthy of them may lead to their subsequent misuse.

8. PI
Joining together

K'an over K'un
Water over the Earth

The Image
Water, everywhere over the earth, flows to join together. A single natural law controls it. Each human is a member of a community and should work within it.

The Judgement
Joining together with others brings success but a group must have a leader. The leader must, however, be a person of exceptionally good character and stability. If we ourselves are not equal to the task, we should join someone who is. If we doubt our ability, the I Ching will guide our choice. If the decision is delayed too long the opportunity, both to lead or to join, may pass us by. The benefits of working together with others will then be lost.

The Lines
6 in the 1st
Be sincere in all your contacts with people, good fortune will then come to you.

6 in the 2nd
The wise person carries out his duties correctly, but he does not blindly follow orders merely to seek favour. Thus dignity is maintained.

6 in the 3rd
Beware of the company of those with whom you do not share spiritual harmony. Being too close to such people will prevent you forming better relationships.

6 in the 4th
It is sensible to show support for a leader, but foolish to be led astray from one's true feelings.

9 in the 5th
A true leader has no need to force others to join him, nor to punish those who do not. Honesty and integrity guide others to a leader.

6 in the 6th
To hold back from the right course of action means that the opportunity is lost. Regret must follow.

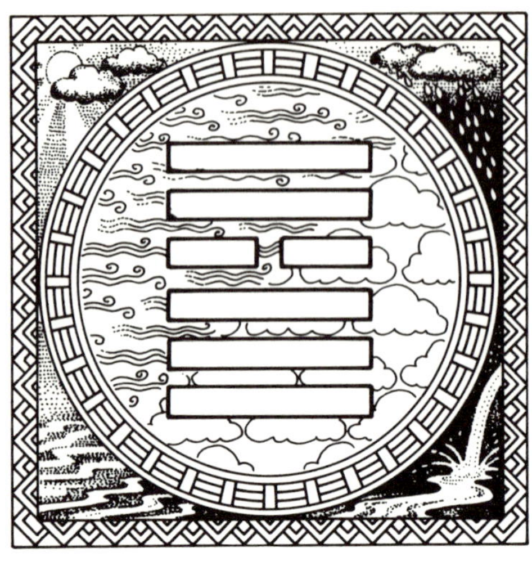

9. HSIAO CH'U

Gentle Progress

Sun over Ch'ien
Wind over Heaven

The Image

Wind, which itself has no substance, can bring together clouds in the sky but they may move apart again. A good person, in difficult times, may likewise only be able to achieve small things.

The Judgement

Conditions are not yet right and we cannot rush ahead to achieve the final objective. Success will come but there are still problems to be solved. The way forward is to proceed gently, adapting to the outside influences, but never weakening our resolve for the final goal. The thoughts and actions of others can still be ameliorated by our influence.

The Lines

9 in the 1st
When the way forward is obstructed and no progress can be made, do not force the issue. Return to the starting position and you can make a fresh advance.

9 in the 2nd
If we see that the progress of other good people is blocked there is no point in pushing forward ourselves. Needless exposure to failure has no value.

9 in the 3rd
Good thoughts and actions may not always bring success against apparently slight opposition. The weak and inferior may prevent progress, so there can be no easy victory. Compromise.

6 in the 4th
The advice given to those in higher positions should always be that which is truly right. This may not be welcomed at first but the inevitability of truth eventually triumphs.

9 in the 5th
Strong and weak people can make friends together, if they are both honest in their approach. Sharing between those who complement each other leads to happiness.

9 in the 6th
When success has been gained, little by little, it should be treated carefully. Taking unfair advantage at this time would not be favourable. Everything may disintegrate.

10. LU

Correct Conduct

Ch'ien over Tui
Heaven over a Lake

The Image

Heaven, by its very nature, is more exalted than a lake. Likewise, with humans, there are differences between people. A system in which positions of authority correspond to inner worth will be accepted but an unfair system produces strife.

The Judgement

When the strong and the weak come together there may be problems. The weak can achieve success, even in such a difficult situation, if the approach is well prepared and pleasant. Antagonism is then not aroused.

The Lines

9 in the 1st

Progress from a low position should be made only to achieve something and not merely to escape from that position. There is no evil in simplicity. Work quietly to achieve success.

9 in the 2nd

The wise man can follow the correct path through life, if he makes no demands and is not led astray by tempting offers.

6 in the 3rd

A weak person who believes himself to be strong brings disaster to himself by reckless action. Only if the cause is extremely just should we risk beyond our abilities.

9 in the 4th
If inner resolve is strong, then success will be achieved, even if the approach is cautious.

9 in the 5th
Determined effort must be made to overcome a problem, but note should always be taken of the dangers which may occur.

9 in the 6th
We are known by the fruits of our labours. If our conduct has been good in the past, we may expect success in the future.

11. T'AI
Harmony

K'un over Ch'ien
Earth over Heaven

The Image
When the influences of heaven and earth combine all things are possible. To achieve success, however, this infinity of prospects must be approached in an orderly fashion. To promote full development the right actions must be synchronized with Natural Laws.

The Judgement
When people and things are in the correct relationship an harmonious existence is possible. When the good are powerful and in charge, then the evil will submit to good influences and themselves improve. These favourable changes are now taking place.

The Lines

9 in the 1st
When things are going well an able person can encourage people to develop themselves. Good influences spread out and everybody achieves more.

9 in the 2nd
Achievement should not lead to limited self-interest among the prosperous. The wise man seeks out and develops the good in all people. Even difficult tasks must be attempted if they are the correct ones.

9 in the 3rd
It is an inexorable Law of Nature that bad must follow good, that decline must follow a rise. To feel that we can rest on our achievements is a dangerous fallacy. Inner stength can overcome anything that occurs outside.

6 in the 4th
When all people feel secure, the successful can mix, freely and easily, with those who have not achieved great things.

6 in the 5th
When the high and the low are brought together they must not accentuate their differences, but instead act together for mutual development.

6 in the 6th
The good times are passing away. They cannot be restored by aggressive actions. Remain true within your own small sphere of influence.

12. P'I
No Progress

Ch'ien over K'un
Heaven over Earth

The Image
When the influences of heaven and earth become separated progress is not possible. Even a good person cannot succeed but must withdraw from public life and work quietly in the background.

The Judgement
When evil people begin to gain control the progress of the good is obstructed. Orderly development is not possible and chaotic conditions emerge. This does not mean that principles should be weakened. They should remain firmly, but quietly, held.

The Lines
6 in the 1st
Because public achievement is not possible, the good draw together in private to await better times.

6 in the 2nd
Weak people will follow both good and bad leaders. The strong person is prepared to suffer outwardly to retain his inner strength.

6 in the 3rd
If a person rises beyond his capabilities he will at first deny this. Inwardly, it cannot be disguised and this is a hopeful sign for the future.

9 in the 4th
When the period of decline is reaching its end, the people who can improve the situation will find themselves called to power. A person who merely imagines himself great may stumble and fail.

9 in the 5th
When good fortune is taking over from the bad, there is still need for caution. Overall success is coming but some ideas may fail. One must try to avoid complacency.

9 in the 6th
Although order will naturally decay to disorder, a positive effort is required to end a period of stagnation and lack of progress.

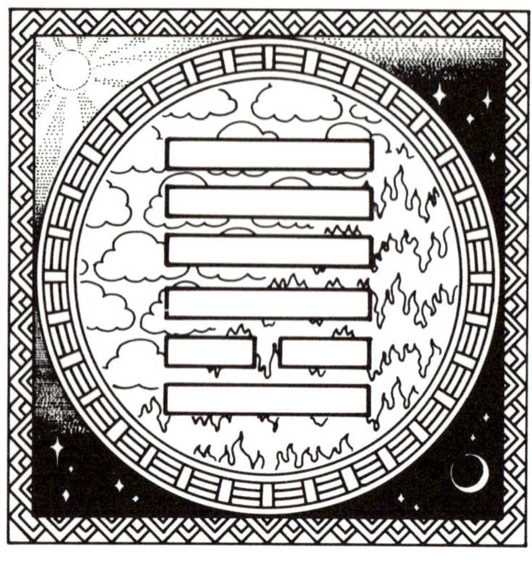

13. T'UNG JEN
Friendliness

Ch'ien over Li
Heaven over Fire

The Image
Although the flames reach up to heaven the two are quite distinct and if they mixed together chaos would result. Likewise, fellowship among men is not due to mingling together but to an ordered, co-operative action. Society is an organized relationship, people acting firmly together but prepared to yield, on occasion, as individuals.

The Judgement
Fellowship is not based upon the trivial interests of the individual. Great things can be achieved by joining with a wise, inspired leader who can clearly see the wider goals of mankind and pursues them without hesitation.

The Lines

9 in the 1st
Open meetings in which all can participate lead to greater things. Meetings behind closed doors will have bad results.

6 in the 2nd
Beware of forming small exclusive groups which are held together only by base motives and a dislike of others. Such groups must inevitably disintegrate.

9 in the 3rd
When one person begins to mistrust another he starts to lay plans to

trap his supposed opponent. Inevitably, he suspects that his former companion is doing the same and the split between them becomes ever wider.

9 in the 4th
A quarrel has now passed its peak. Although the differences of opinion are still as great, they have brought the protagonists to a point where further action would be self-destructive. Common sense must now prevail.

9 in the 5th
Enforced separation causes people who are united at heart to follow hard and difficult paths through life. Eventually they will join together and joy then spreads throughout their lives.

9 in the 6th
There is no reason to feel sad because everybody is not in harmony. If we have, without selfish motives, joined even a small group then something has been achieved.

14. TA YU

Greatness

Li over Ch'ien
Fire over Heaven

The Image

The sun in the sky shines out and has power over all things on earth. Yet each day can bring forth both good and evil. A wise person is modest when in a position of power and can then achieve greatness.

The Judgement

Much good fortune is indicated. Strength is tempered with modesty and clarity of vision. Fate determines when such favourable periods occur.

The Lines

9 in the 1st

Recently acquired wealth or position must not be an excuse for waste and arrogance. Remember the dangers of such excesses.

9 in the 2nd

Help is available to assist with an important task. Forward movement can be achieved when things and people are suitable for the labour ahead.

9 in the 3rd

A great person is always ready to place his possessions at the service of others. To hold on to things, which could be used to benefit others, prevents progress.

9 in the 4th
It is a dangerous situation to be among those who are richer and more powerful. Mistakes may occur through envy and the desire to emulate them.

6 in the 5th
It is not only those who possess great things that will have good fortune. Others will be won over by a sincere and dignified exposition of the truth.

9 in the 6th
Modesty and a desire for truth, if kept by a person of great authority and wealth, ensure that all actions have good fortune.

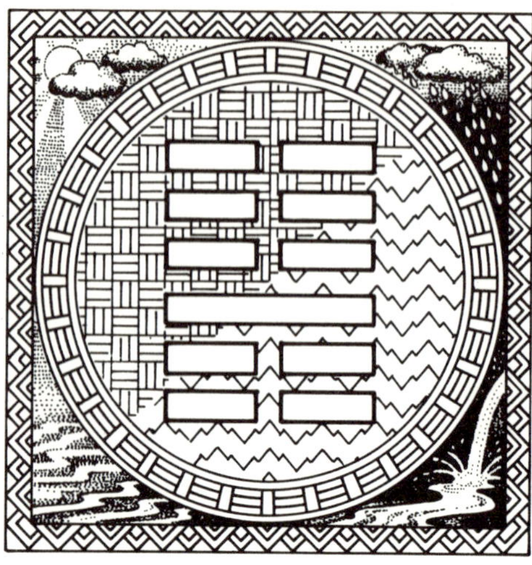

15. CH'IEN
Moderation

K'un over Ken
Earth over Mountain

The Image
When the earth is raised up and the mountain is lowered they form an easy complement to one another. Thus moderation in both makes the gap between the high and the lowly person smaller and promotes equality.

The Judgement
The Laws of Nature are such that things at their peak must decline and those at their lowest point must rise up, just as the sun and moon follow one another ceaselessly through the skies. Man also follows these Laws. A modest man in either a high or low position will achieve his task without seeking attention.

The Lines
6 in the 1st
The modest man can achieve great things. He does not make strong demands on others, nor is he held back by counter-claims. He acts simply and easily and meets no resistance.

6 in the 2nd
A modest mental attitude will show itself in deeds. Nobody can object to this and a beneficial, long-lasting effect is produced.

9 in the 3rd
A modest person, who does not allow fame to upset him, will be able to carry through his plans to the end without opposition.

6 in the 4th
Modesty is shown by carrying out one's responsibility both to those above and those below. It does not mean avoiding responsibility or failing in one's duty.

6 in the 5th
At times, even a modest person must take severe measures. He does not take pride in power. He carries out that which is necessary, without insulting his associates.

6 in the 6th
A modest person does not shrink from responsibility to himself or others. When energetic action is needed it is carried out properly.

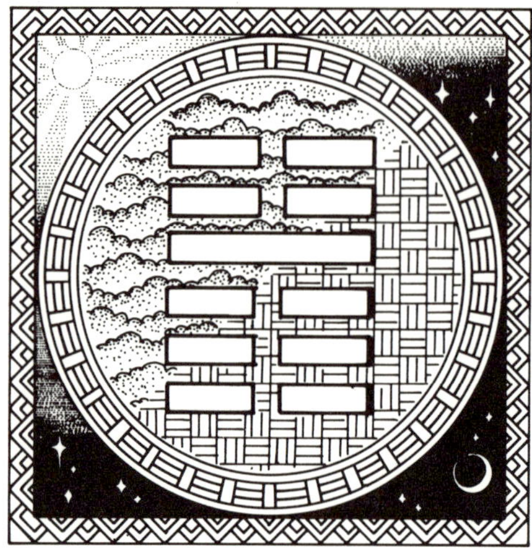

16. YU
Inspiration

Chen over K'un
Thunder over Earth

The Image

When thunder comes it relieves the tension and promotes positive action. Music may do the same by making people enthusiastic and united together. When used to promote good it brings them closer to heaven.

The Judgement

When the right person appears he can arouse enthusiasm and great things, which follow the Natural Laws, will be achieved. With good help and popular support, success can be achieved.

The Lines

6 in the 1st
Those who boast of their powerful friends bring misfortune upon themselves. Enthusiasm must be an outgoing influence which joins people together.

6 in the 2nd
The wise person does not flatter those above him nor belittle those below. In this he remains firm, but is able to perceive the beginnings of good or bad fortune and immediately acts in an appropriate manner.

6 in the 3rd
Enthusiasm must be acted upon at the right moment. Too great a reliance on the guidance of others may cause delays and sorrow.

9 in the 4th
A sincere and enthusiastic person can fill others with confidence so that they may all act together and achieve great things.

6 in the 5th
There are times when forces which prevent action can be beneficial. Energy is conserved for future use.

6 in the 6th
Over-enthusiasm may blind a person to the truth. If, at the end, the error is seen and better action taken, then no great harm may be done.

17. SUI
Disciples

Tui over Chen
Lake over Thunder

The Image
Thunder does not rage all the time. At the appropriate time it is quiet. In the same way, a wise person does not wear himself out by constant action and struggle. There are times when rest and recovery are essential. If necessary, adapt to a difficult situation.

The Judgement
To lead others, a person must first know what it is to follow and then seek willing agreement rather than use coercion or trickery. The cause must be just, both when we lead and when we follow others, if the outcome is to be successful.

The Lines
9 in the 1st
A good leader takes account of the views of his followers but does not allow them to compromise his own principles. He does not merely listen to those who agree with him, but is happy to consider all opinions.

6 in the 2nd
The choice of companions is vital to success. Good friends will aid progress but bad ones will hinder it.

6 in the 3rd
When the right path has been found a person must follow those who

can help and leave those who would hinder. Take care, however, that the path is always true.

9 in the 4th
When a person takes the lead, he may become surrounded by those who follow only for their own self-interest and not for the good of the cause. A good leader, knowing in his own heart what is right, will not be adversely affected by such associates.

9 in the 5th
Place your faith in that which you feel is right. It may be followed without harm.

6 in the 6th
An old sage may prefer to keep his own company after long years of service to others, but if he is properly approached may come again to their assistance and develop close and lasting links.

18. KU
Restoration

Ken over Sun
Mountain over Wind

The Image
Wind blowing around the base of a mountain causes damage, just as base behaviour damages people – all are guilty and corrupted by it. The wise person must stir up interest and promote proper action to correct these evils.

The Judgement
In the present case wrong actions have caused the problem and so right actions may remove it. The task is not easy, however, and must not be rushed into. Careful thought is required first and the project seen through to a stable situation at the end. Firm action, at the right time, is essential.

The Lines

6 in the 1st
The old traditions may have resulted in decay. A carefully planned change will restore stability.

9 in the 2nd
Where problems arise due to weakness, the cure should be gently applied to avoid unnecessary damage.

9 in the 3rd
When it is necessary to correct old problems it is better to be a little

over-enthusiastic than the reverse. Some slight regrets may arise but these should not be a cause of great concern.

6 in the 4th
When things are seen to be going wrong because of past failures, events must not be allowed to take their natural course. Such weakness will have bad consequences.

6 in the 5th
When the problems of the past are so great that one person cannot alone correct them, the help of others will aid progress towards a better situation.

9 in the 1st
It is not necessary for every great person to participate in world affairs by actively involving himself in its progress. If the aim is to set standards above the daily level, that will inspire people for the future, such withdrawal is justified.

19. LIN
Going Forward

K'un over Tui
Earth over Lake

The Image
The earth and the waters upon it sustain all life, their scope is boundless. So the wise person can sustain others with inexhaustible advice and encouragement. No person is too insignificant to be considered.

The Judgement
The time is now favourable to make progress and action should be taken. Remember, however, that less favourable times must inevitably come, just as Autumn must surely follow Summer. Misfortune can be avoided if the proper precautions have been taken early.

The Lines

9 in the 1st
Good influences are beginning to prevail and worthy people are coming forward. Good fortune will come if we remember to keep to what is right.

9 in the 2nd
The call to go forward comes from high places and the wise and resolute person can progress. There need be no worry that things will not always be so good. The path through life inevitably progresses up and down.

6 in the 3rd
When things are going well it is all too easy to become overconfident and not give proper attention to one's duties. If this tendency is recognised early it may be corrected and no harm will be done.

6 in the 4th
When those in authority are open-minded a person of ability can be drawn into high and powerful places without regard to lowly origins.

6 in the 5th
A person in authority must have the ability to attract to himself those people to whom he can confidently delegate responsibility. They must also be allowed to act unimpeded.

6 in the 6th
The wise person who has passed beyond the mundane things of life may need to return, on occasion, to help others achieve good fortune. There is no harm, nor compromising of principles, in this.

20. KUAN
Consideration

Sun over K'un
Wind over Earth

The Image

As the wind blows over the earth it bends the grass to its will. In the same way a great person is able to influence people far and wide. From a true knowledge of their feelings, he will be able to inspire the people, acting as an outstanding example to them.

The Judgement

Those who understand the Laws of Nature and have faith in the World and themselves are able to influence others without effort. Contemplation of those things which are superior expresses itself in a great person's actions.

The Lines

6 in the 1st

A leader of men must carefully contemplate upon his decisions so that he may successfully carry out his responsibilities. For lesser people, who benefit from the wise man's influence, such deep understanding is not necessary.

6 in the 2nd

Those who are in lowly positions do not need to contemplate deeply on matters of wide concern. Those who are in positions of authority must consider the welfare of others as much as their own.

6 in the 3rd
Viewing events in our life from a personal standpoint alone, does not allow a proper evaluation of ourselves. We should consider the effects of our influence on others and then we can properly judge whether or not we are making progress in our life.

6 in the 4th
When a wise person is found, who knows how to promote progress, he should be allowed to act unfettered and not merely considered a useful minion.

9 in the 5th
A person in authority must be constantly examining the effects of his actions. When these are good the decisions are free from blame. Brooding over faults is of no benefit.

9 in the 6th
A great person can free himself of personal restrictions and contemplate, instead, the Laws of Nature. Thus he learns that living without sin is the true way to success.

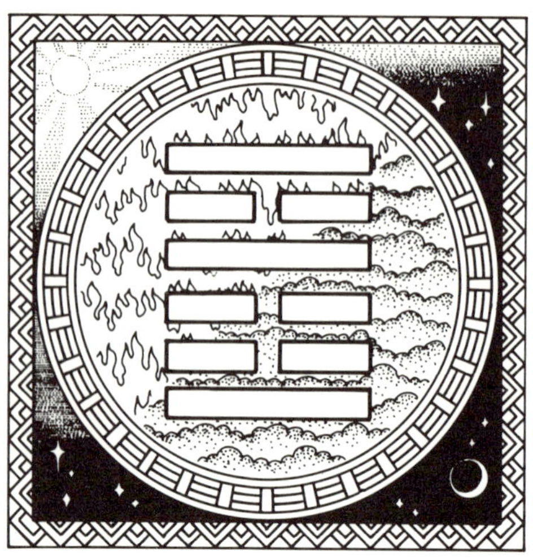

21. SHIH HO

Overcoming Difficulty

Li over Chen
Fire over Thunder

The Image

Before a thunderstorm there is a build-up of tension which is only relieved by the explosive force of thunder and lightning. In human affairs there must be a clear distinction between the penalties for small and great crimes. Retribution for wrongdoing must be swiftly and surely applied if greater problems are to be prevented.

The Judgement

To overcome deliberate obstructions strong action is required because they will not disappear of their own accord. Such punishment must be applied clearly, but not harshly, so that it indicates a proper respect for duty by those in a position of power.

The Lines

9 in the 1st
At the first signs of wrong action, mild steps should be taken to halt the downward path.

6 in the 2nd
In some cases it is easy to distinguish between good and bad and act accordingly. Sometimes, however, one may over-react to something and give a harsh punishment. This should not be a cause for worry because the punishment was deserved.

6 in the 3rd
Wrongdoers do not submit to any but the most powerful authorities. Old problems are particularly difficult to resolve and in carrying out just punishment bad feelings develop against a person who is merely doing his duty. There is no reason to regret such proper action.

9 in the 4th
Great difficulties and powerful enemies have to be overcome and this can only be achieved by strong and resolute action. In time, there will be success.

6 in the 5th
A difficult, but clear-cut, decision must be made. By remaining aware of the responsibility for a perfectly fair solution, mistakes can be avoided and any tendency to leniency corrected.

9 in the 6th
Some foolish people cannot see the error of their ways and carry on along the path to misfortune without thought for the future.

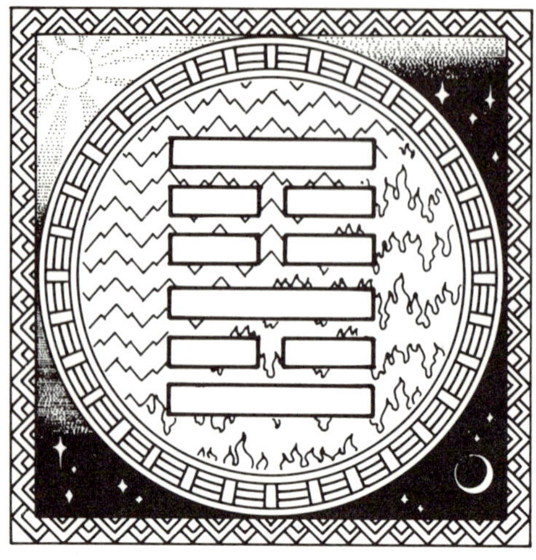

22. PI
Beauty

Ken over Li
Mountain over Fire

The Image
A mountain can be shown in all its beauty by a fire which illuminates it. Likewise, small problems can be clarified and solved simply, by the easy application of the correct solution. Important problems require much more attention.

The Judgement
Beauty in nature and the affairs of Man is a wonderful thing and can promote small successes. Alone it does not have the strength and endurance to achieve the great. The contemplation of graceful harmony, however, allows progress in all things.

The Lines

9 in the 1st
When progressing on a difficult path others may suggest improper ways of making quick progress. The wise person spurns such apparent short-cuts to success.

6 in the 2nd
Outward bodily beauty is nothing without inner beauty. To cultivate the exterior alone is merely vanity.

9 in the 3rd
Drink and good company can be pleasant but must not be allowed to cause idleness. Success depends on steady, thoughtful, action.

6 in the 4th
At times it is difficult to decide between outward success and inner tranquility. A true friend will be able to lead one to simple peace of mind.

6 in the 5th
There is humility in rejecting the opulent for the adequate. Any wise person will accept sincerity instead of lavish appearance and rich gifts.

9 in the 6th
Perfect inner beauty will shine through without the need for external embellishment. Its simple perfection is appreciated without ornament.

23. PO

Disintegration

Ken over K'un
Mountain over Earth

The Image

A mountain rests firmly on the earth but this is a stable situation only so long as its base rests broadly to support the summit. In the affairs of Man, when those at the top grow too high and sharply separated from the rest of humanity, the weakness at the base of society will cause the whole of the society to slowly crumble. A broad and generous base is necessary for survival.

The Judgement

The less able people are crowding in and pushing out the better. This is, from time to time, inevitable. The wise person does not try to bring about great changes but works away quietly, submitting, but not succuming, to the downward trend.

The Lines

6 in the 1st
Evil people are at work destroying those who support a good superior. At present, nothing is to be gained by trying to save them and one can only wait for better times.

6 in the 2nd
Bad influences are all about and one's own position is seriously threatened, without hope of help from above or below. Adjusting to the situation, rather than persisting with a lost cause, is the only way to survive.

6 in the 3rd
If one is in bad company the unseen help of a wise friend can provide inner strength to avoid falling into the evil ways of those around one. They will resent this, but their reaction is only to be expected.

6 in the 4th
Unfortunately, a moment of misfortune cannot be avoided – it can only be endured.

6 in the 5th
The bad have now reached a position so close to the control of power that they can see the benefit of wise action and are ready to take good advice. Good progress will now become possible.

9 in the 6th
When a rotten fruit has finally disintegrated, strong new seedlings grow up in its place. So the evil influences have destroyed themselves and the good, which alone can exist in its own right, is able to grow again to its proper position.

24. FU
Turning Back

K'un over Chen
Earth over Thunder

The Image
Thunder is building up its strength beneath the earth. Energy and robust action must be allowed to build up slowly from a difficult period, which is now passing. Premature action must not be undertaken.

The Judgement
The cyclic change of all things is now, inevitably, bringing about a time of increase. There is no need to rush this along artificially by drastic action. Things will come in their own time – just go forward with the current trend.

The Lines
9 in the 1st
It is not possible to avoid all bad thoughts and deeds, but they must be rejected as soon as they are discerned. Return quickly to the correct path and all will be well.

6 in the 2nd
Never be afraid to turn back from a bad path. Admit the error and follow the example of good people around one.

6 in the 3rd
Some people find it difficult to keep on the right path and keep slipping into bad ways. Although this indicates the need to strengthen personal

resolve it is not a definitive rejection of the good and there is thus still hope.

6 in the 4th
When a person finds himself moving along with bad company he will benefit from taking the advice of a good friend. The rewards of this correct action will inevitably come.

6 in the 5th
If something has been done which is wrong there will be no regrets if this previous action is rejected. There is no benefit in making trivial excuses.

6 in the 6th
There is a proper time for giving up bad ways. If this is obstinately refused then misfortune must inevitably come.

25. WU WANG
New Beginnings

Ch'ien over Chen
Heaven over Thunder

The Image
The life-force of thunder resounds in the heavens and new life is awakened. At this early stage it has not yet been corrupted and acts in accord with the true Laws of Nature. There is respect for all forms of activity and thought, each nurtured towards its own true ends. Even the unexpected may occur.

The Judgement
Behaving in the manner of natural action and justice brings success in what is right. Following the corrupted path brings misfortune.

The Lines

9 in the 1st
The first actions which our heart tells us to take may be followed confidently. Good fortune will come.

6 in the 2nd
Each task should be undertaken as and when it is due, without thought for future benefit. Success comes from doing each job properly.

6 in the 3rd
In all matters, unexpected losses at the hands of others will sometimes occur. If we acquaint ourselves with current situations, such misfortunes may not occur.

9 in the 4th

Good things cannot be lost, especially when lavished on others. If we remain true to our own good natures and do not allow others to corrupt us, then there is no cause for worry.

9 in the 5th

When undeserved evil falls upon one there is no need to take drastic action to remove it. The force of good will, in its own time, prevail.

9 in the 6th

When fate is against one and the time is not ripe for action, nothing can be achieved. Wait quietly, without resentment, for the right time.

26. TA CH'U
Justified Progress

Ken over Ch'ien
Mountain over Heaven

The Image
The creative treasures of heaven are hidden safely within the mountain. The wise person acquaints himself with the words and deeds of the past and applies them to the present, so that his actions may have greater effect.

The Judgement
The time is favourable for carrying out bold public schemes. The wise have been given positions of trust and can make progress in great enterprises. Personal integrity will enable even the most difficult tasks to be completed.

The Lines

9 in the 1st
Although a good person wishes to make progress he is being firmly held back. Forcing the issue brings misfortune, so it is better to await the right time for action.

9 in the 2nd
The restraining forces are so strong that no action can be taken at the present time. Build up resources quietly for future progress.

9 in the 3rd
The obstruction has been cleared and one can go forward under the

guidance of a wise leader. There are, however, still dangers and to progress one must have the right skills and an eye open, both for unexpected problems as well as the goal.

6 in the 4th
A strong force is growing but easy success can be achieved if steps are taken early to direct this powerful influence.

6 in the 5th
Dangerous forces exist that can cause harm by rushing forward. They should not be confronted but instead directed towards better ends by internal changes.

9 in the 6th
Success is now granted to those who deserve it. Energy and effort can be applied to solve difficult problems.

27. I
Moderate Attitudes

Ken over Chen
Mountain over Thunder

The Image
Thunder at the base of the mountain brings conditions favourable for growth. The wise man shows moderation in his eating and drinking, thus providing a healthy base for his words and deeds, which also reflect his tranquil and moderate attitudes.

The Judgement
The true nature of people is shown by their actions. A correct attitude to both oneself and others promotes success. Cultivate the right actions, so that good may come of one's efforts.

The Lines

9 in the 1st
If one looks with envy and resentment at the situation of others it will lead to a loss of self-reliance and freedom.

6 in the 2nd
It is proper for those who are unable to look after themselves to be cared for by others. When, however, capable people fail to support themselves because of wrong attitudes, this is not right and unless they mend their ways misfortune will come.

6 in the 3rd
Seeking only personal pleasure and the unceasing satisfaction of desire

can never lead one to true happiness. This erroneous route leads only in a circular path, never going forward.

6 in the 4th
There is no harm in an insatiable desire for the right helpers to assist in worthy projects. Such efforts are not self-centred and promote true development.

6 in the 5th
It may be found that one's duty is beyond one's capabilities. If this is admitted there is no harm, for the help of others, who are hiding their true worth, will bring success. Beware, however, of forgetting this dependence and attempting things which cannot be achieved.

9 in the 6th
Those with great ability also have a great responsibility. If this is humbly remembered, then even the most difficult tasks can be carried out to everybody's benefit.

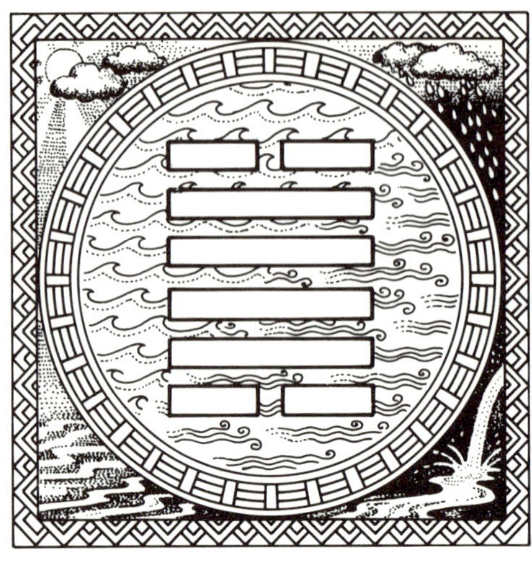

28. TA KUO
Easy Progress

Tui over Sun
Lake over Wind

The Image
In exceptional times water may be raised up beyond its proper level. This represents a great store of power which cannot, however, last for ever. So the great man exerts influence over the world but is not regretful when this peak has passed away.

The Judgement
The great and wonderful are clearly in existence. Such a situation cannot last for ever and the wise person takes gentle action to prepare for the changes ahead. Force is not required, merely proper preparation.

The Lines

6 in the 1st
When an exceptionally difficult task is to be undertaken it is essential to prepare very carefully for it. With cautious beginnings there will be no need of remorse later.

9 in the 2nd
In exceptional circumstances the unexpected becomes likely. New vigour and life abound, small new beginnings bring success.

9 in the 3rd
When things are going well, it is easy to disregard the sensible advice of others and take on too much. Without help the burden will become too great and the enterprise collapse.

9 in the 4th
With the assistance of those below him, a wise man can overcome problems and everybody will benefit. If the good advice is misused for personal gain, however, the outcome will not be good.

9 in the 5th
When there is no real inner strength left in a person or thing it is not possible to achieve great results. Clinging to the old and familiar, trying to extract the last vestiges of activity from them, can only hasten their decline. The outcome is inevitable because no renewal is possible.

6 in the 6th
In difficult and dangerous times it is often necessary to risk all to do what is right. If, in the attempt, all is lost there can be no blame – the cause was just and the action necessary to ensure that good will ultimately prevail.

29. K'AN

Overcoming Problems

K'an over K'an
Water over Water

The Image

Water flows ever onwards to its ultimate goal, bringing life to every place it touches. Likewise, a great person proceeds steadily with his duties, encouraging the good in all people and things. Dangers and difficulties do not deflect him from his task.

The Judgement

No matter how steep a drop or dangerous its path, water never changes its essential nature. In Man's affairs sincere and truthful appreciation of a problem allows the correct response to be naturally adopted. Difficulty and danger can protect against the faint-hearted – those with true worth will not be deflected from their purpose and will pass through it without harm.

The Lines

6 in the 1st
Living with danger and evil can easily lead to a disregard for what is right. Such lapses will inevitably bring misfortune.

9 in the 2nd
In dangerous times it is not possible to obtain immediate overall success. The situation must be carefully considered and small gains accepted. Be content not to be overwhelmed.

6 in the 3rd
When the situation is so difficult that no way, either back or forward, is

safe, it is essential to remain calm and accept the problems. A path to release will eventually appear.

6 in the 4th
When there is danger all around, we should drop all pretentions and concentrate on the simple, sincere, acts which give mutual assistance. Start at the small point of clarity and truth, letting influence spread out naturally from there.

9 in the 5th
When conditions are difficult it is not possible to achieve really great things. Instead, the wise person takes the line of least resistance, to allow him eventually to reach his true goal.

6 in the 6th
When a person completely loses all respect for what is right and becomes ensnared in evil, he is unable to escape from the great dangers around him. Misfortune is then certain.

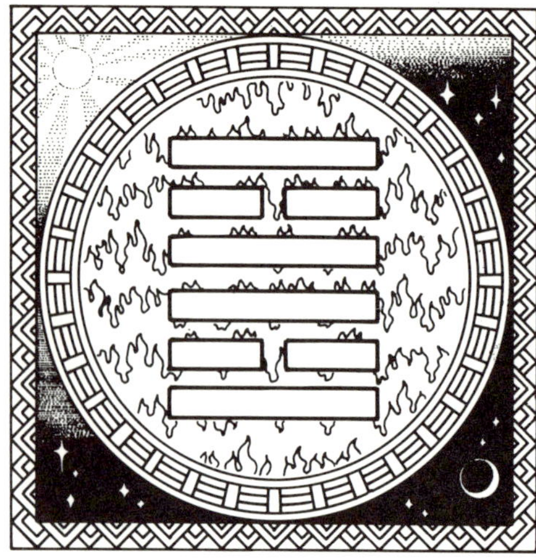

30. Li
Luminaries

Li over Li
Fire over Fire

The Image
The sun pours out its light and illuminates the whole of the natural world. The light clings to objects and makes them brilliant. In the same way great people illuminate all those around them, penetrating to the true nature of Man.

The Judgement
Those who radiate wisdom and truth can only continue to do so if their inner strength is based on what is right. By observing the Laws of Nature and behaving in accord with their directions, man finds his true place in the world. No person is free of such influences in their life and success is only possible when actions are in accord with them.

The Lines
9 in the 1st
At the beginning of the day all manner of conflicting duties crowd in. It is important to consider the start carefully and with proper composure so that what follows will be orderly and successful.

6 in the 2nd
If we hold to the true middle course, then success is assured. Good will be created.

9 in the 3rd
The great person does not lament the passing of his life. He does not

spoil the experience by frittering it away in the idle pursuit of pleasure nor regretting its shortness. Ensure that what is achieved has followed the true path to immortality.

9 in the 4th
Bright fire clings to wood but consumes it in the process, leaving nothing of lasting worth. So may a brilliant but unrestrained man shine quickly but become spent too soon.

6 in the 5th
When the peak of life has been reached it is a time to discard vain hopes and fears for the future. Consider and lament on what has passed, so that a change for the better may prevent premature exhaustion.

9 in the 6th
When evil is being overcome it should be rooted out and destroyed at its very centre, but there is no need to destroy those who have merely been led astray. In the same way it is best not to be excessive in controlling one's own harmless faults, while treating the serious ones.

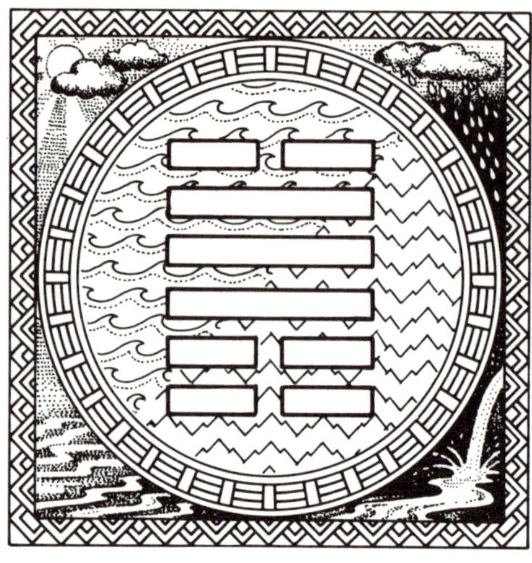

31. HSIEN
Complementary Influences

Tui over Ken
Lake over Mountain

The Image
A flat-topped mountain has a lake at the top which provides moisture for its slopes, instead of merely rising bleakly upwards. People are always ready to give good advice to a humble and receptive person. Mutual influences between people are beneficial, as they are, for example, between man and woman.

The Judgement
Success depends on the balance between complementary influences. In the relationship between man and woman neither must dominate the other because excesses cannot yield happiness. In like manner, the great person can influence the lesser and vice versa.

The Lines
6 in the 1st
An idea which exists only in the mind of one person has no influence until it is expressed. Then it may lead to good or evil.

6 in the 2nd
If an idea or action is not yet ready to be carried out, because it is incomplete, then the matter must be delayed or self-injury may occur.

9 in the 3rd
It is essential that one's own actions be restrained. There is no merit in

carrying out either one's own or another's whims. In affairs where the heart rather than the mind rules, it is essential to realize the possibility of limiting action at some times, to allow true freedom at others.

9 in the 4th
When strong, heart-felt emotions are involved it is essential that they are backed by a steadfast character which does not seek merely to influence, for its own gain, those around. Incitement of specific people limits the ability to influence others and eventually leads to personal exhaustion.

9 in the 5th
The ability to truly influence others arises unconsciously within oneself. The internal strength to control our own actions influences the actions of others.

6 in the 6th
Mere talk, without the heart behind it, can only produce superficial results. Others will not be deeply influenced by it.

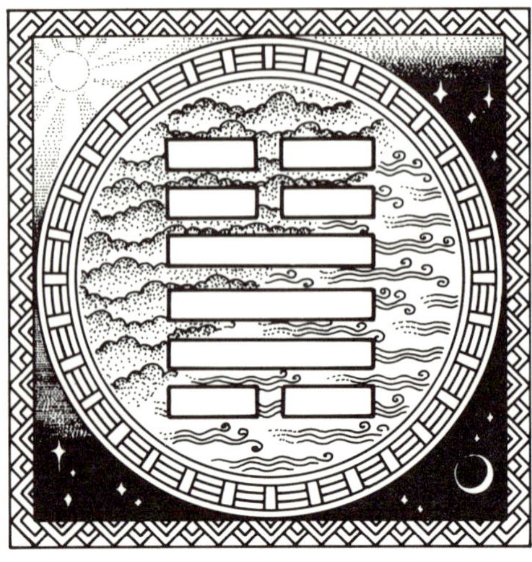

32. HENG
Perpetual Progress

Chen over Sun
Thunder over Wind

The Image
The gentle wind blowing and the sound of thunder are apparently labile, insubstantial things, but in their constancy of interdependence and certainty of return they are enduring influences. Likewise, the great person is flexible to changing times, but retains an inner direction which does not vacillate with the moment.

The Judgement
In all things that achieve and endure, there is ceaseless motion. Endings are new beginnings, the cycling of natural phenomena an everlasting progress. The wise do not stagnate but self-renew at every stop.

The Lines
6 in the 1st
Easy deeds and quick rewards do not endure. True success requires careful thought and preparation.

9 in the 2nd
When inner strength exceeds outer resources it is necessary to hold back. No cause for concern over excessive action will then arise.

9 in the 3rd
The wise follow their inner strength to prevail over external problems. To allow external forces to shape one's actions invites misfortune. Unexpected problems are not prevented by fear of their occurrence.

9 in the 4th
If we are to achieve success we must act in the right way. Effort alone is not sufficient – it must be directed towards a proper objective.

6 in the 5th
Those who take a responsible and active role in the affairs of the world must remain adaptable and flexible to its just demands. Those with lesser aspirations may follow a less difficult route.

6 in the 6th
Ceaseless activity which never settles anything is a dangerous tendency for those in authority. There are times when affairs must be consolidated.

33. TUN
Conserving Resources

Ch'ien over Ken
Heaven over Mountain

The Image
As mountains reach skyward, so the heavens retreat before them. The great person does not hate those who are less worthy, for that would bind them together. Instead, he remains superior. His strength cannot be assailed by those who fall short of his ideals.

The Judgement
At a time when irresistible adverse influences are starting to be felt, it is essential that a proper plan be adopted for controlled retreat. This is not weakness, for it retains strength rather than wasting it in a hopeless struggle. The way is thus prepared for future advance.

The Lines

6 in the 1st
If ordered action is not being taken to withdraw from a difficult situation, it is better to remain quiet than to adopt panic measures.

6 in the 2nd
In difficult times, those who can hold firmly to what is right and keep wise company will survive the problems.

9 in the 3rd
When lesser people are holding back a reasonable line of action and are preventing an escape from difficulty, it will be sensible to allow them to

come under your influence. This may not allow the accomplishment of great things but will avoid the alternative of falling entirely under bad influences.

9 in the 4th
When the wise person departs from bad company he loses nothing. It is the bad company which suffers from the lack of his wisdom.

9 in the 5th
The wise person knows when it is necessary to retreat. He does so in a friendly way, but is firm in his convictions – nothing will be gained by hesitating over trivial matters.

9 in the 6th
When all ties with a difficult situation have been severed, then the right course of action is clear. Inner strength guides directly to the good.

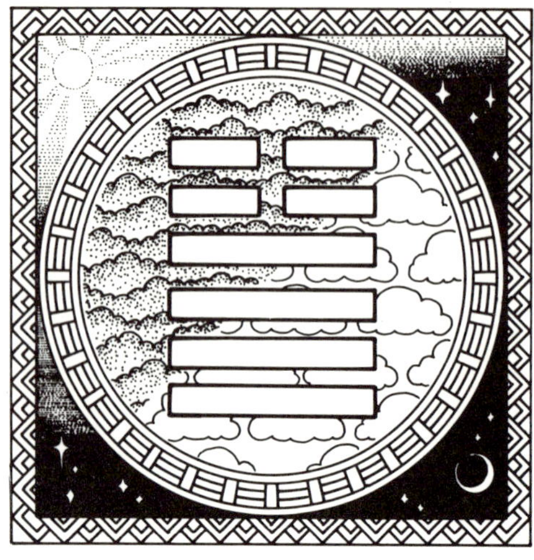

34. TA CHUANG
Justified Action

Chen over Ch'ien
Thunder over Heaven

The Image

The proper place for the power of thunder is in heaven. Then things are as they should be. Likewise the great person is always in total harmony with what is right and his actions have good effects.

The Judgement

When great power exists it is all too easy for it to degenerate into mere personal force, acting without proper consideration for the circumstances. Only power applied to a just cause can bring success.

The Lines

9 in the 1st
When those in lowly positions have great power they are tempted to use brute force to advance their position. Misfortune will come from such misuse of the situation.

9 in the 2nd
When good fortune is just beginning it is easy to push forward too quickly. Careful consideration and preparation are still necessary.

9 in the 3rd
A foolish person in possession of power seeks to achieve everything by its use and this is not possible. A wise person uses force only when it is right and does not boast of his superiority.

9 in the 4th
Great resistances can be overcome by the slow and methodical application of what is right. There may be no outward display of strength since all is concentrated internally to yield success.

6 in the 5th
When things can be easily achieved there is no need to use force. There need be no remorse for acting gently.

6 in the 6th
At certain times it is impossible to go forward and trying to do so merely creates more difficulty. The wise person appreciates this fact and by changing course is eventually able to succeed.

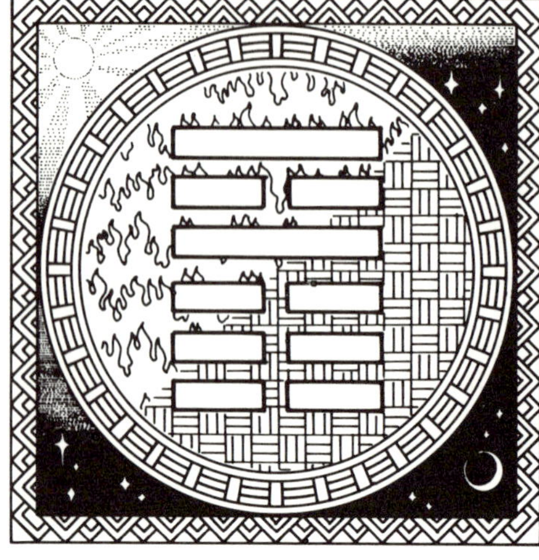

35. CHIN

Successful Development

Li over K'un
Fire over Earth

The Image

As the sun rises its influence becomes ever brighter. The virtue of a great person grows ever stronger as the corrupting influences of mere earthly life are overcome.

The Judgement

The wise person is able to influence his equals and direct their efforts towards successful actions. He does not do this for his own glory, but for the attainment of even greater goals. Thus, those in higher positions of authority do not become jealous of his achievements and all are able to work together in harmony.

The Lines

6 in the 1st

When everybody is pressing forward it may not be clear which lines of action will bring success. In such a situation one should calmly continue with what is right, not trying to force the support of others or becoming angry at their refusal. Then there will be no cause for remorse.

6 in the 2nd

Sometimes it proves impossible to contact a great person who can help with a problem. This is sad but should not discourage effort. Eventually the justified reward will come and everybody will be seen to have acted properly.

6 in the 3rd
To make progress the assistance of others may be essential. This is no reason to regret one's own limited abilities, which require such help.

9 in the 4th
When developments are taking place it is always possible for those in key positions to gain, for themselves, personal benefits. This is clearly not right and such defects of character will eventually be exposed.

6 in the 5th
In progressive times a person in a position of influence may feel that he should take personal advantage of the situation, rather than remain steadfastly to what is right. Such temporary regrets about gains or losses are not significant, for his benefits are in being able to achieve success by good influence.

9 in the 6th
There are times when aggressive actions are necessary to correct the mistakes of those around one. Such actions have their dangers and over-use will lead to misfortune.

D

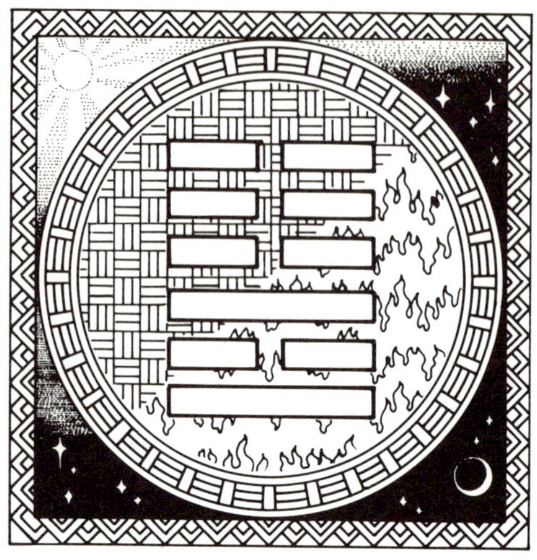

36. MING I
Outer Darkness

K'un over Li
Earth over Fire

The Image
The light of the sun has vanished beneath the earth and darkness reigns supreme. At such times, when the evil influences are ruling the earth, the wise man also hides his light. He does not extinguish it but must allow many unsatisfactory things to pass by. To seek to expose evil will bring misfortune, but one must remain true.

The Judgement
In difficult circumstances a great person must outwardly remain yielding but inwardly cling firmly to his principles. Only by this hidden perseverence will ultimate success be achieved and major adversity be overcome.

The Lines

9 in the 1st
In difficult times a good man may try to rise above problems but only meet more hostility. In order to remain true to his principles he will have to suffer greatly and be forsaken by others around him. His fixed aim will, however, sustain him.

6 in the 2nd
In bad times the good may suffer personal injury, but if they continue working for the benefit of others this will ultimately lead to good fortune.

9 in the 3rd
Apparently by chance, victory is achieved over evil influences. Success is assured but action must not be taken too rapidly. It takes time to correct long-standing problems.

6 in the 4th
Close acquaintance with inferior persons in positions of great power may reveal that there is no hope of changing them for the better. In such cases there is no alternative but to remove oneself quickly before misfortune occurs.

6 in the 5th
Where escape from external evil is impossible, the great person must possess an unshakeable faith to survive the inevitable deprivation and be extremely cautious in all his visible actions.

6 in the 6th
At the peak of its influence, when all good has apparently been overcome, the forces of darkness consume themselves and their influence wanes.

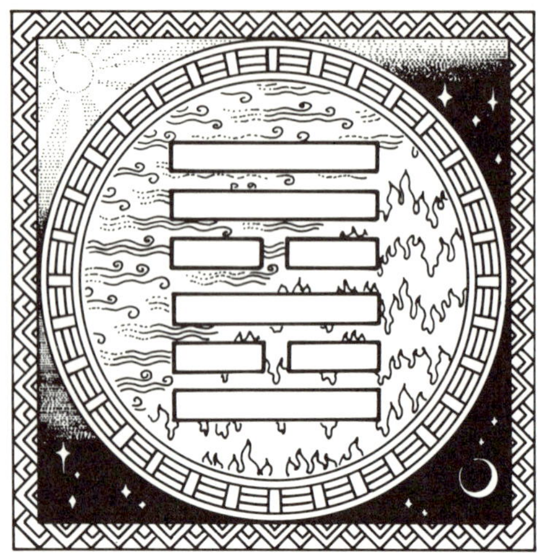

37. CHIA JEN
Relationships

Sun over Li
Wind over Fire

The Image
Energy from the heat of a fire stirs up the wind. Such forces arise from within and are based upon a continuing supply of fuel. In the close relationships between people, as in a family, communication is only successful when words and deeds relate together. The power to influence others is based upon a firm constancy arising from inner faith in what is right.

The Judgement
In the family group, or other close relationships, it is the correct behaviour of one person to another, founded on obligations and loyalties, that brings success to the partnership. When extended beyond the small group, such attitudes promote successful business and social activities.

The Lines

9 in the 1st
Relationships must be based on a firm application of the rules of proper conduct. In all matters there is a need to curb unsatisfactory behaviour at the earliest opportunity, otherwise the transgressions grow larger. Get things onto a satisfactory footing as soon as possible.

6 in the 2nd
Everybody has a duty to others which they should carry out to the best

of their ability. It is not proper to take over other's tasks by force and neglect one's own proper role in life. Even the most menial act is a corner-stone to family and social life.

9 in the 3rd
In relationships a proper balance must be struck between rigidity and laxness. There must be scope for freedom of action but the limits of this must be clearly defined. The situation where anything is acceptable leads to disorder and unhappiness, both within and outside the family.

6 in the 4th
Good fortune depends upon a proper attention to duties. The stability of a family, a business or a government, depends on good housekeeping.

9 in the 5th
The influence of a person who can be trusted is not to be feared. Of itself, it will direct others to right actions.

9 in the 6th
The ability to accept responsibility and create order depends on personal character. If inner truth shines out, success will eventually be achieved.

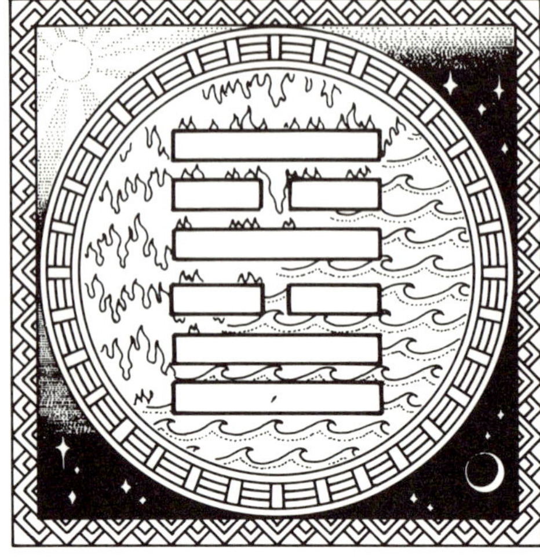

38. K'UEI
Differences

Li over Tui
Fire over Lake

The Image
Although a fire may burn on the waters of a lake the two elements never mix together. A good person among the bad still retains his integrity. Beauty is unaltered by the presence of ugliness, opposites are not lost by co-existence.

The Judgement
When opposition and non-communication prevent great progress, one should move forward gradually rather than meet difficulty head-on. In itself, difference of opinion and position are not bad things, for it is by the proper consideration and resolution of differences that progress is made. The joining of opposites, as of man and woman, allows the achievement of great things.

The Lines
9 in the 1st
When opposition occurs it is pointless to try and produce harmony by force. If it is a close companion, they will return of their own accord. If it is evil from outside, it will pass away provided we ourselves do not follow the bad example.

9 in the 2nd
When open strife occurs between people, who at heart believe in the

same things, progress towards harmony may be made by informal contacts.

6 in the 3rd
It often seems that no progress can be made and that others are against all good ideas. This is not a reason to be led astray but rather to cling more tightly to what is known to be right. In the end the wise person will find himself amongst his own kind.

9 in the 4th
When among those who do not follow the same true path it is inevitable that one will feel isolated. Meeting a trustworthy person who holds similar views removes the dangers of isolation and allows progress.

6 in the 5th
Under conditions of estrangement from those around, a person of like mind may not be recognised at first sight. When his true motive is revealed, one should approach and work together.

9 in the 6th
Sometimes it is one's own inner feelings which misunderstand the motives of others. Preparations may be made for defensive action where none is necessary. If such a personal fault is recognised and overcome it will be possible for good to come of the meeting.

39. CHIEN

Hindrance

K'an over Ken
Water over Mountain

The Image

With dangerous water before and steep mountains behind there are obstacles all around. An inferior person blames his problems on others, but the great person searches his own heart for errors and, by tackling them, strengthens his own character.

The Judgement

An obstruction prevents all forward progress. The wise person halts and joins the company of others, taking good advice to heart. The inner resolve, however, is not reduced and the new approach brings success.

The Lines

6 in the 1st
When a severe obstruction to progress occurs it is foolish to rush blindly forward. Consider the situation and conserve energies for successful action at the right moment.

6 in the 2nd
It sometimes happens that one's duty to others forces one to enter difficult situations. Although other actions might be easier there is no blame in undertaking difficult tasks in this case.

9 in the 3rd
When faced with great difficulties, which would be hazardous to tackle, the wise person must be mindful of those who depend upon him. It

would be irresponsible to leave them undefended and unprovided for. Turning back will bring happiness.

6 in the 4th
Some obstacles cannot be overcome alone and to try to do so will bring failure. It is sensible to take more time and gather able assistance so that success is certain.

9 in the 5th
In difficult times a person may be called upon to tackle dangerous problems. If he has the strength of character to undertake the task, he will be able to call upon willing helpers, who can assist in overcoming the obstacles which exist.

6 in the 6th
When a problem arises it is often found that a wise person who could solve it has already moved on. He could say it was no longer his concern, but a great man can never do this. His duty requires him to assist and his ability enables him to bring good fortune to others. In a time of crisis such help should be sought.

40. HSIEH
Liberation

Chen over K'an
Thunder over Water

The Image
Thunder brings rain which clears away the tension existing before the storm. The wise person acts in the same way when clearing up difficulties created by men. When success is achieved there is no need to dwell on errors, whether accidental or intentional.

The Judgement
When a difficult problem is overcome, it is sensible to get back to normal as soon as possible rather than overdo the forceful action which has achieved success. Any small problems remaining should be dealt with quickly, so that the clean new start can stimulate good fortune as soon as possible.

The Lines

6 in the 1st
When a problem has been overcome there is no need for further words and deeds. Quiet recovery is all that is needed.

9 in the 2nd
When false friends of those in positions of power seek to turn them from the true path, they must be hunted down and removed with all one's strength. Perseverance against evil brings good fortune.

6 in the 3rd
Those who have recently acquired rich goods or high position often do

not know how to conduct themselves under such circumstance. They flaunt their new-found power and invite misfortune, both from those above and those below.

9 in the 4th
In times when little thought or action is required, even a great person may become surrounded by inferior people who support him. When difficulties have to be overcome, however, the wise person frees himself of such acquaintances and seeks the companionship of persons of truly like mind, so that together they may achieve success.

6 in the 5th
The great person is able to detach himself from bad influences by his inner strength. Then, those who are not worthy of his company see that they really have nothing in common with him and move away. This occurs even when all other methods of removing them have failed.

6 in the 6th
In some cases inferior people in positions of power do not see the error of their ways. Under such circumstances the wise person must prepare himself for the task and then act to bring about deliverance from evil.

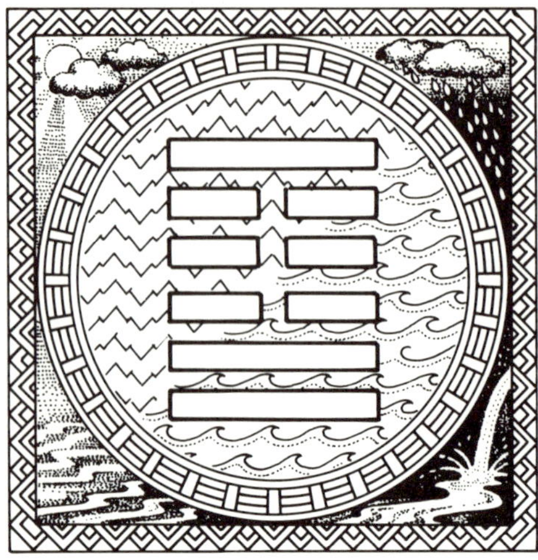

41. SUN
Deficiency

Ken over Tui
Mountain over Lake

The Image
When a lake evaporates its waters can then enrich the bare mountain above rather than rush bubbling from the lake when it overflows. In the same way it is necessary for people to curb their natural instincts and develop their inner selves, so that a balanced personality may develop.

The Judgement
There are times when resources may not be available for grand acts and schemes. Then there is no misfortune in behaving simply, for the inner richness will still be expressed in its true form.

The Lines

9 in the 1st
When one's own duties have been carried out, it is good if help is given unselfishly to others. The wise person, however, takes care that he does not receive excessive help, for that would diminish the relationship. Both helper and helped must be sensitive to the situation.

9 in the 2nd
To truly help others it is necessary to retain your freedom of action and self-esteem. To slave for another without thinking causes harm to self and gives no lasting benefit to others.

6 in the 3rd
A person alone will easily find a companion when something is under-

taken. Close relationships are possible between two people, but between three problems will always arise.

6 in the 4th
One's personal faults may be aggravated by external circumstances. If a sincere attempt is made to overcome one's own faults others will perceive this and extend their friendship. Others will hold back if you, yourself, are not well motivated.

6 in the 5th
Some people are born lucky and this is abundantly clear to others. Good fortune will attend everything such people do.

9 in the 6th
There are those whose every success brings benefit and not loss to others. Through hard and continuous effort, such people achieve great things and always find willing helpers to assist them. Acting in such a way brings good fortune to everybody.

42. I
Mutual Benefit

Sun over Chen
Wind over Thunder

The Image
Wind and thunder mutually strengthen each other. Every person has the ability to improve himself. Seeing good in others their actions can be imitated. Seeing bad in oneself this can be eliminated. In these ways character can be strengthened.

The Judgement
Those in positions of power should make sacrifices for the benefit of those below. In this way people have faith in their leaders and are prepared to co-operate with them to achieve great things. Times for successful action, however, do not last for long and must be made use of when they exist.

The Lines
9 in the 1st
When unexpected assistance comes to a person this should be used to achieve things which would otherwise have been impossible. In moving forward in this unselfish way great good fortune can be produced.

6 in the 2nd
True improvement in a person can only be achieved by developing inner desire for that which is right. Then desired objectives are attracted of their own accord and no obstacle can prevent them. Good fortune must not be an excuse for forgetting one's principles, but must be taken properly to heart and used accordingly.

6 in the 3rd

In times of great achievement and success it is possible for even difficulties and failures to turn out to be advantageous. By acting properly, even greater inner strength is developed and good influences produced, as if by legal proclamation.

6 in the 4th

It is to the good of everybody that there are unselfish and just people who act as intermediaries between leaders and the main mass of people who follow. In this way good influences are spread both upwards and downwards, to the benefit of all. This is especially important when great tasks have to be carried out.

9 in the 5th

A person who is truly of kind heart does not need to proclaim this fact. His deeds will speak clearly for themselves.

9 in the 6th

It is the duty of a leader to help those following. If this is not done the followers will not support the leader when he makes demands upon them. Instead his enemies will draw closer because people will not be in harmony.

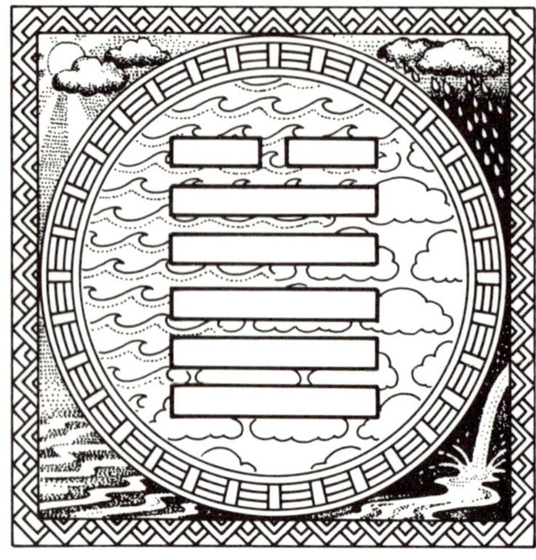

43. KUAI
Overcoming Evil

Tui over Ch'ien
Lake over Heaven

The Image
When a lake has risen to the top of its shores or its water has all evaporated into the skies, the subsequent release of this water must be expected, by flood or rain. If one stores up riches only for oneself, then loss must also become certain. The wise person spreads his wealth, even while he is accumulating it. He continually examines his own motives, ensuring that he is always following the right course of action and has not become blind to the needs of others.

The Judgement
One bad person can spoil the efforts of many good people and one bad thought can spoil the benefits of many good ones. To overcome evil one must be resolute in its condemnation, but not adopt direct confrontation using the weapons of evil. Promote, instead, all that is good, both within and without. Finding no hatred to flourish in, evil will wither away.

The Lines
9 in the 1st
When we are about to undertake a difficult task it is important to take stock of our own strength first. If we go beyond its limits an early defeat is likely and the whole may then be lost.

9 in the 2nd
The wise person is ever aware of the possibility of danger and harmful

influences around him. He does not fear them, for he is prepared by his inner strength to overcome problems. People will respect and follow such a resolute, but sensibly cautious, leader.

9 in the 3rd
When everybody else is crying out against injustice it is very difficult not to join them. The cause of justice, however, may be served by keeping some contact with foolish people, provided one does not allow them to contaminate the inner self. Such actions will be misunderstood, but a person with true strength of character can endure such problems.

9 in the 4th
Many people want to achieve great things but find their path continually blocked. The greater they struggle the more difficult things become. Such people obstinately refuse to take the only sensible advice – to cease from vain conflict and allow things to take their true course.

9 in the 5th
As every gardener knows, it requires constant struggle to overcome weeds. In a similar way a good person in a lowly position will have a constant struggle with lesser people who have gained positions of authority. One must remain resolute in the face of such problems and so retain inner strength of character.

6 in the 6th
Evil, both within oneself and in others, is very difficult to overcome. Even when complete success appears to have been achieved, we must be on our guard for tiny remnants of evil which will later grow out again. Be thorough in attention to detail.

44. KOU
Influence

Chi'en over Sun
Heaven over Wind

The Image
The wind blows under the heavens, spreading out in all directions. In the same way a leader influences all those around him by his commands, setting into action even people whom he does not know.

The Judgement
It is important for success that mutually complementary people come together. This must be done in the right spirit, however, because if someone who is good weakens his principles to meet a lesser person, that would be unfortunate. One should never underestimate possible dangers.

The Lines
6 in the 1st
If a small amount of error is seen to have crept into something it must be firmly tackled at once. If anything which is wrong is left alone it will grow stronger and ultimately cause problems.

9 in the 2nd
Bad influences should be kept under gentle and not repressive control. Great care must be taken, however, that they do not contaminate others and thereby allow evil to grow in strength. If this is done, no harm will occur.

9 in the 3rd
There is always a temptation to adopt bad habits. One is fortunate if cir-

cumstances prevent this. This may make it difficult to act in the right way, but if we see the dangers then greater misfortune will be avoided.

9 in the 4th
It is worthwhile to cultivate the friendship of people who appear of no great significance at the present time. Later, one may need their help and it would be our own fault if they did not then give assistance.

9 in the 5th
A wise leader is able to rely on his own strength of character to influence others who are in lesser positions. It is not necessary for him to give pompous displays of power, nor to be constantly complaining of their actions. They will respond to this freedom and show their respect for his integrity by following his directions.

9 in the 6th
When a person has removed himself from the daily affairs of other men, he will often find their attention troublesome and send them away roughly as beneath his concern. Others may dislike him for this, but it is of little importance because he has no longer any need of contact with them. Provided their attitude does not upset him, no serious harm will be done.

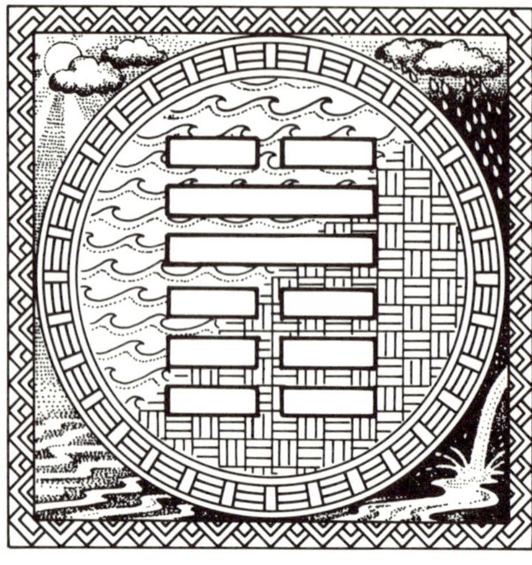

45. TS'UI
Co-operation

Tui over K'un
Lake over Earth

The Image
A lake has gathered the waters together and holds them over the earth. In such situations there is always a danger that the waters will break out and cause damage. When people and possessions are gathered together there are dangers of personal disagreements and of loss by robbery. The wise person prepares himself for all possibilities and so avoids misfortune by being able to act quickly.

The Judgement
When people gather together a natural leader is needed. For the family one can look towards its present head and to the achievements of those who have in the past contributed to it. For affairs of business and state a common faith is necessary to unite efforts behind a wise leader. Great success is then possible by combined action.

The Lines

6 in the 1st
When people are in a group all sorts of possibilities will exist and it is difficult to decide which is the right path of action. When the need for leadership is clearly seen, a wise leader will be found who can guide them. If they follow his advice all will be well.

6 in the 2nd
When people are gathering together in groups it is important not to join

them without thought. The heart will give strong advice on which to choose. In this way we need have no fear of joining the wrong group, nor any need to make elaborate preparations to join. Even the smallest offer of help is appreciated if made to the group in which, by spirit, we truly belong.

6 in the 3rd
A newcomer may find it difficult to join an already existing group and be upset at not being readily accepted into it. If this is so, one should collaborate closely with someone who is already well established in the group. General acceptance will come later.

9 in the 4th
A wise person, working for the good of others, will be able to gather helpers around him so that his efforts are successful. Because his reasons are not selfish, there will be good fortune.

9 in the 5th
A person in authority will naturally gather others around him. He will be able to use his influence to promote good projects but will need to take great care to win over those who are not fully committed to his ideals. Only strength of character and good example will achieve this.

6 in the 6th
If co-operation with another is desired, but one's help is not accepted, it is right to be sad. Seeing the real sorrow that results may then influence others to adopt an attitude of fruitful collaboration.

46. SHENG
Achievement

K'un over Sun
Earth over Wind
(Wood)

The Image
Trees grow up from the earth, finding their way relentlessly, but without undue haste, around all obstacles as they reach upwards. Likewise, the great person progresses resolutely, step by step, along the right path to achieve ultimate success. (Note that in this hexagram SUN takes its alternative meaning of 'wood'.)

The Judgement
The time is favourable for seeing people in authority and pushing forward actively with projects. This should not be done, however, with aggressive force but by unassuming hard work, adapting as necessary to the situation. Good fortune is assured.

The Lines
6 in the 1st
The strength of character and hard work needed to achieve great things often starts from simple and humble beginnings. If this good is recognized by those above and mutual confidence is inspired, then success will come.

9 in the 2nd
A person with great strength of character may not fit easily into his present position in life and not act in accord with other's expectations of him. Provided his heart is true, such minor deficiencies are of no real importance.

9 in the 3rd
The time is very favourable. Everything attempted easily brings success and no problems are visible. At times like this one should not worry about future problems but instead concentrate on moving forward. Such times do not last forever.

6 in the 4th
This is a time of great achievement. Objectives of lasting worth can be achieved because one is accepted and acclaimed by all men and thus given a position enabling great good to be done.

6 in the 5th
As progress is made and one achievement follows another, it is all too easy to become careless and attempt steps which are too large. Remain humble and maintain steady progress, with attention to detail. In this way ultimate success is reached.

6 in the 6th
One should not push blindly forward looking only to the final end as this causes one to overtax one's strength. Remember to act with consistent attention to every small detail, progressing step by step.

47. K'UN
Subjection

Tui over K'an
Lake over Water

The Image
The water has completely drained from the lake, leaving it empty and incapable of anything. When external forces and conditions make it impossible for a person to carry out successful actions, nothing can be achieved. The wise person looks inwards, remaining true to his own self in such difficult times.

The Judgement
Even in times of adversity, when nothing is able to make progress externally, the wise person can build up inner benefits. He does not become despondent, but stores up inner strength so that later success will come. He does not waste his wisdom on deaf ears.

The Lines
6 in the 1st
When a foolish person meets great difficulties, he allows them to break his spirit and loses his own sense of direction. The wise person accepts his fate and moves onwards, retaining his inner strength intact.

9 in the 2nd
It is possible for the inner self to be drained even when there appears to be no external problems and one is surrounded by the trappings of success. Help will come which will lead one away from this difficult state, but the journey should not be started before the inner attitude has been set right by a considered strengthening of character.

6 in the 3rd
When a person meets great difficulties it is important not to allow them to break his spirit. To dash repeatedly at the problem will not overcome it. Seeking refuge in people and things that merely deflect one from the proper course of action will only lead to further distress.

9 in the 4th
It often happens that those people in a position to help others do not do so properly. They become diverted by the influence of others and put off by difficulties. Provided the inner strength is present, however, they will eventually overcome these problems and successfully aid others less fortunate than themselves.

9 in the 5th
A good person can sometimes achieve nothing, because those above fail to help him and those below do not support him. At such a time, one must hold to one's inner strength and let things slowly take their own course for the better.

6 in the 6th
The difficulties and failures of the past may make one slow to take advantage of present opportunities. An inner change of attitude will allow forward movement and the yoke of the past can be cast off.

48. CHING
Collaboration

K'an over Sun
Water over Wind
(Wood)

The Image

Trees draw up water from below and wood may be used by man to construct a well for the same purpose. The parts of a plant co-operate in the process of transpiration. A wise person organizes people in a co-operative effort for mutual benefit. (Note that in this hexagram SUN takes its alternative meaning of 'wood'.)

The Judgement

Although external situations and conditions may change, some things go on from age to age unchanged. A well is always based on the same principles, reaching downwards into the earth to bring up life-giving water. If all its parts are in harmony it will function properly. In both the external and inner affairs of Man this is also true. Too much attention to one facet of society or human existence is unsatisfactory. The limitless wells of inner spiritual strength must be kept always in mind and their contents developed to a high level.

The Lines

6 in the 1st

Those who are content with second best and cease to strive for better things lose both their own respect and that of others. If there is no inner strength then there is nothing for people to seek.

9 in the 2nd

If a person possesses good qualities but neglects them, this is like letting life-giving water drain away. Only worthless companions will associate with such a person and nothing can be achieved.

9 in the 3rd
A wise person exists whose knowledge could help others, but those in positions of power do not know of his talents, so his friends are sad. Everybody would benefit from the proper direction of his efforts.

6 in the 4th
There are times when we must set our own house in order to be able later to help others. This inner work is not wasted, for it makes possible greater benefits in the future.

9 in the 5th
The wisdom of great men is like an inexhaustible well. It can accomplish nothing, however, unless it is taken by others and put to good use.

6 in the 6th
A good well never runs dry, no matter how much water is taken from it. In the same way a wise person is never exhausted by the needs of others for his advice. The more that is freely taken by others the greater will be his own store of inner wisdom.

49. KO

Promoting Change

Tui over Li
Lake over Fire

The Image

Fire and water are in inevitable conflict and when brought together must result in mutual destruction. The various seasons, likewise, cannot exist together, but we can recognise order in their continuous changes. In the affairs of Man, too, we can be prepared for changes by anticipating their natural development.

The Judgement

In the affairs of Man and Nature there is Spring and Autumn. If a person's motives are true and the time is right, great changes may be made and everybody will benefit. Not everyone, however, has the strength of character to inspire others in such dangerous times.

The Lines

9 in the 1st

Drastic changes should only be undertaken when all else fails. Great self-control is needed so that useless and premature action is not taken. Consider carefully the problem.

6 in the 2nd

When all forms of gentle persuasion have failed there must come a time when severe action is necessary. Then a true leader must be found, who can inspire the confidence of others. Change must be considered and its consequences prepared for. Good fortune will then come.

9 in the 3rd
It is a mistake to undertake drastic changes too quickly, before the needs and the methods have been properly established. It is also wrong to delay too much when well-justified changes are needed. Consider well the call for, and the need for, change. Only if it is necessary and generally accepted will success come.

9 in the 4th
To promote beneficial change a person requires not only a position of power but also the inner strength to remain true to his ideals. Others will not continue to follow a cause which is based upon selfish instincts.

9 in the 5th
The wisdom of the leadership of a great person is clearly visible to others. He does not need to win their approval, nor look for guidance himself.

6 in the 6th
After a major change for the better in a situation, there will remain small problems which have not yet been solved. The wise person does not seek to overcome all of these at one time. To do so would invite dissatisfaction and consequent failure. Conditions will remain favourable only so long as we continue with what is truly possible, using the help that is presently available.

50. TING
Sacrifice

Li over Sun
Fire over Wind
(Wood)

The Image
Fire continues to burn when it is supplied with fresh wood and stirred by the wind. A wise person finds his true place in life and lives in accord with what fate decrees. His inner strength nourishes his actions and all people benefit from this harmony, just as food nourishes the body. (Here the hexagram SUN implies also its additional meaning of 'wood'.)

The Judgement
The spiritual flame of truly great people spreads out beyond their worldly deeds. That which is invisible and lacks physical substance can endure all material changes, but has no meaning without its influence for the better upon Man's actions. Success comes to those who humbly offer their sacrifices for the greater spiritual good of others.

The Lines

6 in the 1st
Even the person in a lowly position can achieve success if his heart is fixed on what is truly right. Others are ready, then, to accept the fruits of his labours.

9 in the 2nd
When society is in an advanced state it is important that one achieves something of real significance. Others may be jealous of such success, but there is no harm in this if one rests on proved achievements and does not claim more than is justified.

9 in the 3rd
In a complex society a person may find himself in a position where his talents are not recognised and he cannot then show his true ability. The wise person is not worried by this because he knows that, if he has something of real worth, the time will eventually come when he has the opportunity to develop it.

9 in the 4th
It is essential that those with difficult problems to solve have both the ability and the inclination to apply themselves to the tasks. Great works will fail if they are not undertaken by the right people.

6 in the 5th
A good and modest person in a position of power will attract able associates so that they can, together, carry out difficult tasks. Provided the leader retains this humble attitude, further successes are possible.

9 in the 6th
A wise person will dispense his knowledge and wisdom without adulteration. Thus they can be seen by all, both in heaven and on earth, as the rare gifts that they are. Under such circumstances good fortune is assured.

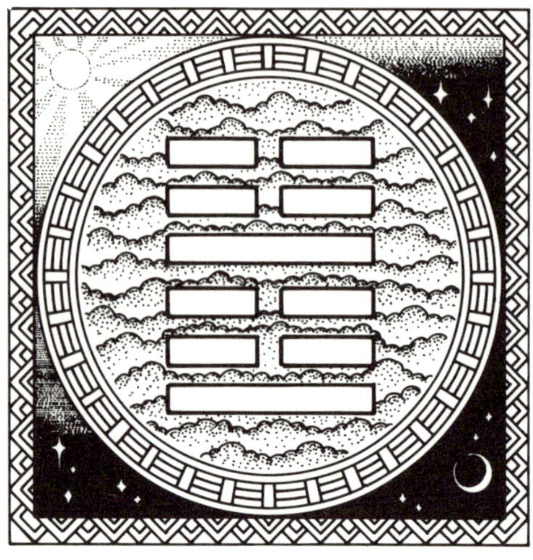

51. CHEN
Fear

Chen over Chen
Thunder over Thunder

The Image
Thunder upon thunder arouses fear and trepidation. The wise person respects such power and ensures that his own heart is free from error, providing a firm base for future development.

The Judgement
When the power of Nature is revealed all men are afraid, but those who have already met fear in their inner hearts do not fall in terror. Such true leaders are not deflected from their duty by personal fears for their own safety.

The Lines

9 in the 1st
When a person first suffers shock and fear he feels himself discriminated against. When the danger has been overcome, however, the inner strength which is gained enables him to succeed in his future activities.

6 in the 2nd
In times of great difficulty and danger a person may lose all his possessions. It would avail him nothing to try to recover them at that time, because retreat from the danger is the only sensible course. Later, he will regain his possessions.

6 in the 3rd
When external fate deals us a blow it is all to easy to lose our initiative

and flounder aimlessly. To succeed, we should allow such difficulties to stimulate action. Then the problems are easily overcome.

9 in the 4th
There are times when even the mind cannot see a way out. If there is no obstacle that can be overcome, nor easy route to success, then no useful action is possible.

6 in the 5th
At some times life deals repeated blows, in quick succession. To avoid loss one must steer a middle course and prevent oneself being deflected aimlessly from the true way forward.

6 in the 6th
When severe shock is able to penetrate to the inner core of a person, he is robbed of the ability to act sensibly. Inner strength to await the proper time for action can only be present in those who are not yet affected. Seeing the errors of others he should draw back to avoid misfortune, even though they are angry with his inactivity.

E

52. KEN
Peace of Mind

Ken over Ken
Mountain over Mountain

The Image
Mountains that are close together remain constant in their relative positions. The heart of Man should emulate the stillness of such natural features. Concern should be for the immediate situation. A wise person does not worry over what might be.

The Judgement
True peace of mind, which is not concerned with the petty struggles of mankind, arises from within. One does not make mistakes when base self-interest is kept from the mind, for one's acts are then in accord with the Laws of Nature.

The Lines

6 in the 1st
At the beginning of any activity one is still free of the influence of conflicting interests and can see the route clearly. Then is the time to pause and carefully consider the enterprise so that the right approach is made. Once found, however, resolute action should then be taken to prevent wandering from the course.

6 in the 2nd
When one serves a strong leader one cannot influence his actions. Even a good friend cannot divert a bad companion from evil ways.

9 in the 3rd
One cannot make people calm by force. Repression brings only other

forms of discontent. A calm mind, likewise, can only develop of its own accord. Enforcing stillness of heart cannot lead to true peace.

6 in the 4th
To reach the highest states of mind one must learn to overcome one's desire for personal glory and gain. At first this can only be done with considerable effort and the influence of self-interest still exists. This state is not a cause for remorse, however, because it is a step in the right direction.

6 in the 5th
In times of stress and danger people tend to talk foolishly and without thought. The wise person remains quiet in such situations and does not say something which he later regrets.

9 in the 6th
When one has acquired a tranquil attitude to the major aspects of life, as well as to its trivial problems, one is in command of oneself. A person is then able to direct all his energies towards successful activities.

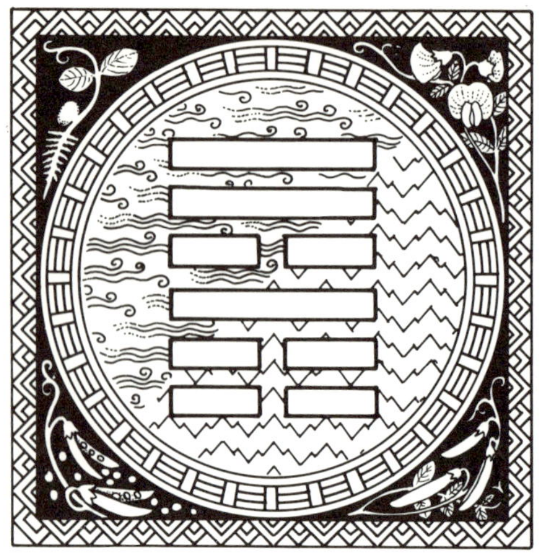

53. CHIEN
Improvement

Sun over Ken
Wind (Wood) over Mountain

The Image
A tree grows slowly on a mountain but its presence affects the whole view. The influence of a wise man also only grows slowly, gradually gaining in external power as his inner strength develops. Sudden rises to power have no lasting effects. (Note that in this hexagram SUN takes its alternative meaning of 'wood'.)

The Judgement
To achieve lasting success in any endeavour a steady, painstaking, development is necessary. Sudden bursts of activity cannot produce effects, either internally or externally, which are of real permanence. Officials must be seen to be properly appointed and collaborative schemes properly organised. When things develop slowly, however, it is essential that the final objective be kept clearly in mind, otherwise there is a danger of ceasing to strive for ultimate success.

The Lines

6 in the 1st
When a person first starts out on a new road in life the way is always difficult, with people ready to criticize but not to help. Initial problems, however, often produce the perseverance of character which leads finally to success.

6 in the 2nd
When early success has provided a firm base, the wise person uses it to

develop further. He does not hoard his good luck but instead shares it with others.

9 in the 3rd
The wise person does not seek conflict or attempt rash actions. He is content to protect what is his own and allow other things to take their natural course. Unnecessary conflict brings misfortune.

6 in the 4th
We often find in life that circumstances beyond our control have brought us to a position which does not suit us. The wise person quietly seeks out a safe resting place, away from immediate dangers.

9 in the 5th
A person who has worked hard to reach a good position may find that those close to him do not understand his actions and so he cannot make further progress. This is often the fault of less worthy people who are currently exerting influences upon his friends and superiors. In time these problems will be overcome and then all will go well.

9 in the 6th
A time eventually comes when something significant has been achieved. Such success is a shining example to others, who by following the same route may also develop their own potential to the fullest extent.

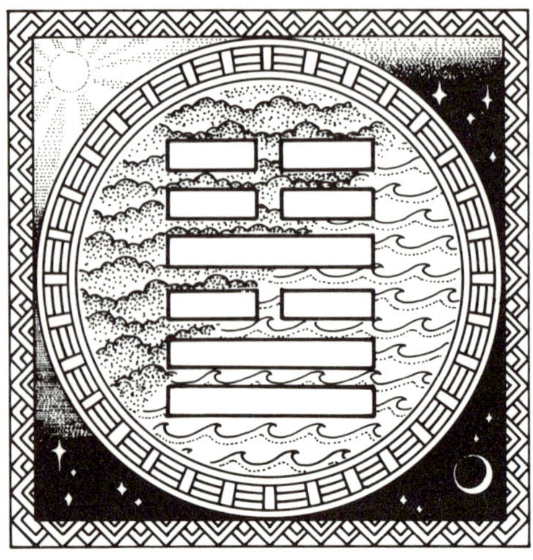

54. KUEI MEI
Good Behaviour

Chen over Tui
Thunder over Lake

The Image
Thunder sounds over the lake and the surface waters are stirred into following ripples. The wise person does not allow his relationships with others to drift along. He always keeps the ultimate aim of a true and lasting relationship in mind and thus avoids unnecessary upsets caused by minor differences of opinion.

The Judgement
Legal and contractual relationships are based on clearly defined positions, but personal relationships always depend upon the behaviour of individuals. Respect for the feelings of others is the basis of all successful human friendships. Without it there can only be inevitable problems.

The Lines

9 in the 1st
Although a person is hampered by not achieving a high position of authority it is still possible to exert a good influence, if one has the confidence of someone who does have the necessary power. The wise person, however, does not abuse this position of trust by seeking to outshine his superior.

9 in the 2nd
In a relationship between two partners both should act in union, like

two eyes together. Even when problems arise in one partner the other should remain loyal to the partnership.

6 in the 3rd
It is sometimes impossible to achieve what one desires on one's own account. In such cases some happiness may be found by joining the service of others.

9 in the 4th
Virtue will in due course bring its rewards. It may sometimes be better to hold out for what is really desired rather than accept a compromise solution.

6 in the 5th
When a person has not yet become dependent upon rich living it is still possible to achieve happiness by accepting a humble position or a subordinate place in a relationship. If this can be done there is a prospect of good fortune.

6 in the 6th
A marriage, or any other partnership between people, will not succeed unless it is entered into whole-heartedly. Without respect between partners there can be no lasting relationship.

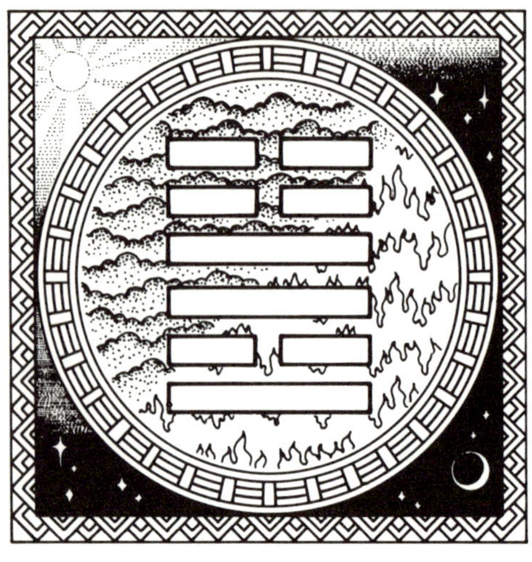

55. FENG
Prosperous Times

Chen over Li
Thunder over Flame

The Image
The sound of thunder surrounds lightning. Inner clarity, which can see things as they really are, is surrounded by powerful action which brings a just solution to problems.

The Judgement
It is a time of great achievement but only a person who is clear in mind and soul can lead successfully. The wise person is not sad because of the certainty of future decline. He rejoices in the present good fortune.

The Lines

9 in the 1st
In a favourable period it is sensible if those with good ideas collaborate with others who have the necessary energy or power to carry them out. Such partnerships, once established, can last as long as conditions are suitable, without failing.

6 in the 2nd
Although the time is favourable, a barrier to achievement has been created by lesser people. This stops useful contact between a person in authority and one who could help him achieve success. The wise follower does not worry about this, for he knows that the inherent value of his assistance will eventually be made clear and bring good fortune to them both.

9 in the 3rd
The true leader has been eclipsed and is unable to achieve anything. Those of little worth shine out in unwarranted brilliance. The wise follower is helpless to assist, but knows that this is not due to his own failings.

9 in the 4th
Towards the end of a period of stagnation people will come together and pool their abilities to achieve success. The actions of those with power and energy will complement the good ideas of others and a time of good fortune will come.

6 in the 5th
When a leader has an open mind he will take the good advice given by others. This will bring a time of good fortune to everybody.

6 in the 6th
To strive, above all else, for wealth and power over others, takes one along a path which has only room for one person. Isolation from friends and family is inevitable.

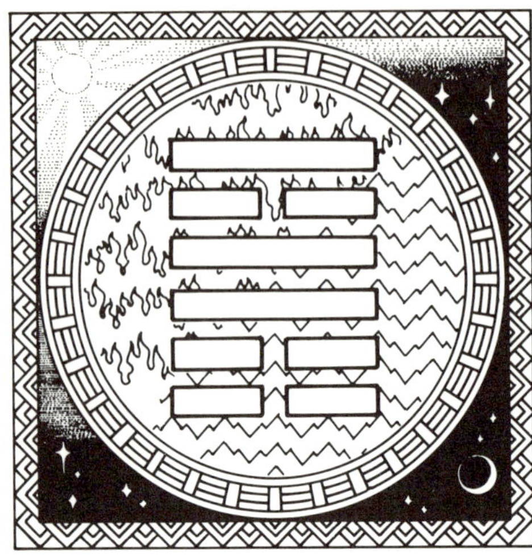

56. LU
The Itinerant

Li over Ken
Fire over Mountain

The Image
Fire briefly lights up the mountain but it moves on from place to place as the fuel is exhausted. The wise man uses punishment in the same way – swift, clear and appropriate in severity to the transgression.

The Judgement
A person who has not made a fixed home among friends and family must give special attention to how he travels. He must give constant attention to the company he keeps and not be surly or arrogant with those he meets. Then he can pass freely from place to place, taking good fortune with him.

The Lines
6 in the 1st
When amongst strangers, it is important to be humble and restrained in behaviour. No one welcomes the humour and jokes of an unknown person. Foolish acts will be considered a sign of a foolish person.

6 in the 2nd
People are happy to help a quiet stranger who clearly acts in accord with high moral principles. Thus he will gain faithful friends and helpers to promote his well-being.

9 in the 3rd
Through arrogance and meddling in the affairs of others a stranger can

easily lose all friends and assistance. To be completely alone in a strange place is not favourable.

9 in the 4th
Even when a stranger is able to control his strong inner desires he may not be at ease. He will be constantly on guard against losing what he has already acquired and this will keep him a permanent stranger to others.

6 in the 5th
If one knows the customs and the correct way of proceeding, it is possible to find a satisfactory position even when away from home. Success will attend the proper approach.

9 in the 6th
A person who is imprudent in word or deed while among strangers will later have cause to regret such foolishness. Always keep your own position in mind when dealing with others.

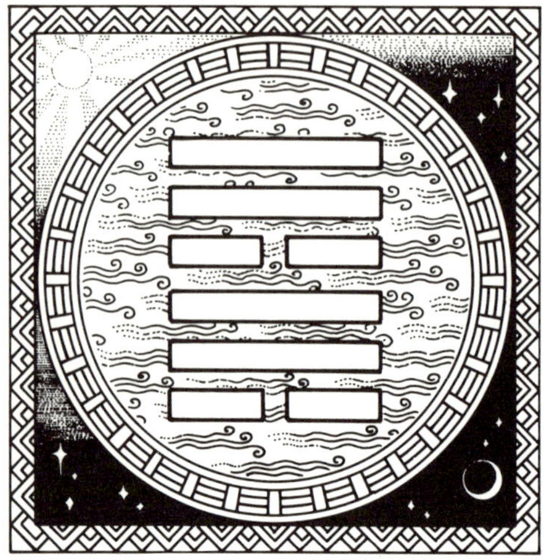

57. SUN
Dedication

Sun over Sun
Wind over Wind

The Image
Winds following one another gently penetrate all corners of the sky. By ceaseless activity all is finally clarified. In a similar way the wise leader knows that his thought must penetrate into every one of his followers if actions are to be successful. People are upset and worried by things which they do not understand.

The Judgement
Although it appears less spectacular in its action the effects of slow, dedicated, application may be more long-lasting than sudden break-throughs. To succeed, however, a wise leader is required who can direct the efforts of dedicated helpers always towards the same end.

The Lines

6 in the 1st
There are times when consideration for others may cause a person to fail in his duty. When the correct path has been chosen it must be followed decisively.

9 in the 2nd
It is often difficult to track down evil to its true source. Such efforts, however, are always worthwhile for when the source is found and made public it ceases to be a problem.

9 in the 3rd
It is bad policy to continue to re-examine every problem after a reason-

able consideration has been given to it. A decision must be taken and acted upon while there is still time if a person is not to be considered ineffectual.

6 in the 4th
The combination of ability with opportunity is a most favourable circumstance. Energetic application of skills which have been painstakingly built up will lead to great success.

9 in the 5th
There is a time when bad beginnings can be made good. Careful thought is needed before action is taken, but then the reforms should be pushed through resolutely. Afterwards, the improvements should be carefully monitored to ensure that the new path is correct. Success may yet be achieved.

9 in the 6th
The desire to eliminate evil is not enough. There must also be the strength to defeat it completely, if one is not to draw danger and harm to oneself.

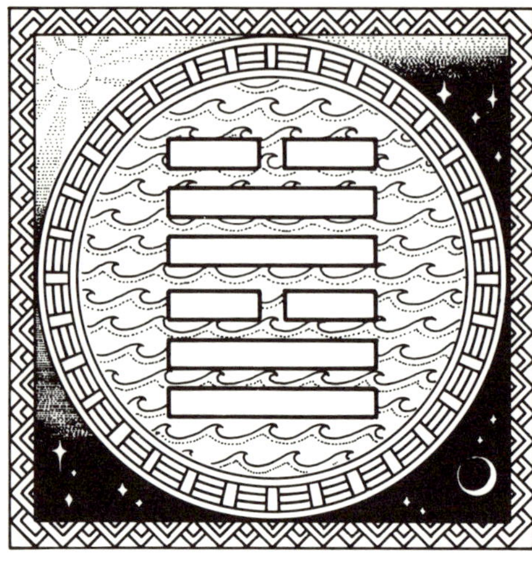

58. TUI

Friendship

Tui over Tui
Lake over Lake

The Image

One lake feeds another, replenishing it as the water evaporates, so that it does not dry up. The search for knowledge is also fuller if more than one person is involved in it. Discussion with friends makes learning a happy experience.

The Judgement

To gain the friendship and help of others one needs an inner strength to follow the path of truth and an outer happiness to encourage all to follow it. This will win more permanent and devoted helpers than any form of coercion, for true friends will take on all manner of difficulties for their companions.

The Lines

9 in the 1st

Those who are truly happy do not need to seek support from outside. Their happiness arises from the inner strength of their own purity of thought.

9 in the 2nd

The wise person only takes part in pleasures which are appropriate to his position. He finds no pleasure in base and degrading activities, even when his present companions are immersed in them. In this way he never has cause for regretting his behaviour.

6 in the 3rd
When a person has no inner worth he seeks, and finds himself surrounded by, idle diversions which have no substance. No lasting pleasure can ever come from such activities, which cause a person to wander, ever more aimlessly, in search of self-indulgence.

9 in the 4th
There is always a choice of diversions available. Only when a person has developed the inner knowledge to choose, unhesitatingly, what is right, will he find true happiness. Unworthy pleasures always bring sorrow.

9 in the 5th
We are all surrounded by dangerous influences which can stealthily corrupt us if we do not recognise them for what they are. The wise person sees the possible harm and acts accordingly, to avoid future trouble.

6 in the 6th
A person who lacks inner strength cannot guide his own life. He is swept along by the whims of external forces, the victim of a pointless search for personal pleasure.

59. HUAN
Overcoming Selfishness

Sun over K'an
Wind over Water

The Image
When a warm breeze blows over frozen waters it melts and disperses the ice, which has been solidified over the winter. When a person's mind has been hardened by selfish desires it is both unable to move of its own accord and yet isolated from the beneficial influence of others. Only the acceptance of a strong new faith can release the spirit from its prison.

The Judgement
The desire to place self above others is a disruptive influence in society. To overcome it, people must be encouraged to co-operate together in schemes which will bring benefits to all. Only an unselfish person, with a true heart, has the power to organize such a beneficial project.

The Lines
6 in the 1st
As soon as problems and misunderstandings arise in a joint enterprise it is essential to take swift action to clear them up. It will then be possible to achieve success.

9 in the 2nd
When we see anger and dislike of others growing in our hearts we must take immediate steps to halt it. There is need at such times to strengthen one's inner faith by whatever is found helpful. The world is seen as a better place when good humour is restored.

6 in the 3rd
Some tasks which are placed upon us are so difficult that we must give up all self-interest in order to carry them out successfully. The strength to do so without regret can be found if the outer achievement is of sufficient worth.

6 in the 4th
When we are working for the general good of society we may need to withold assistance to our immediate friends. Only others who have the wisdom to see beyond their own small place in life can understand that this is right.

9 in the 5th
In a time of problems, when everything seems to be falling apart, there is need for a focal point of activity. By concerted efforts the situation may be improved.

9 in the 6th
When danger threatens family and friends, it is right to lead them away from confrontation so that injury is not inflicted upon them.

60. CHIEH
Limits

K'an over Tui
Water over Lake

The Image
There is a limit to the amount of water which a lake can hold and it is not possible to fill it beyond this limit. Although a man has unlimited possibilities he cannot explore them all. The wise person keeps his spirit free by setting his own limits as to what is right and proper.

The Judgement
To be successful, limits must be set upon all things, because these define the transition from one stage to another. It is prudent to set limits to our consumption and expenditure, for then we are prepared for future changes to less favourable conditions. There is no merit, however, in excessive limitation for its own sake, because this leads to repression and resentment.

The Lines
9 in the 1st
A wise person knows how to live within the limitations imposed upon him and will conserve his strength so that he may act more effectively when the time is right. Current discretion in word and deed allows successful action later.

9 in the 2nd
When the time for action has come there should be no delay. After careful preparation the opportunity should be seized without hesitation.

6 in the 3rd
If a person gives himself over entirely to the pursuit of pleasure and sets no limits to his expenditure, this can only lead to misfortune. If he accepts the consequences as his own fault he will have learnt something that will benefit him in the future.

6 in the 4th
It is a waste of effort to attempt to limit something which, by its own nature, cannot be limited. If we are content to work within natural limitations then we can achieve success.

9 in the 5th
When restrictions have to be made they should apply to oneself first. Others will be happy to follow such a good example without the need for coercion.

6 in the 6th
To persistently impose severe pressure upon people must inevitably force them to strike back, just as too much restriction of diet and comfort disrupts the normal working of the human body. This is not to say, however, that severe measures should not be taken, when necessary, to prevent oneself succumbing to bad influences.

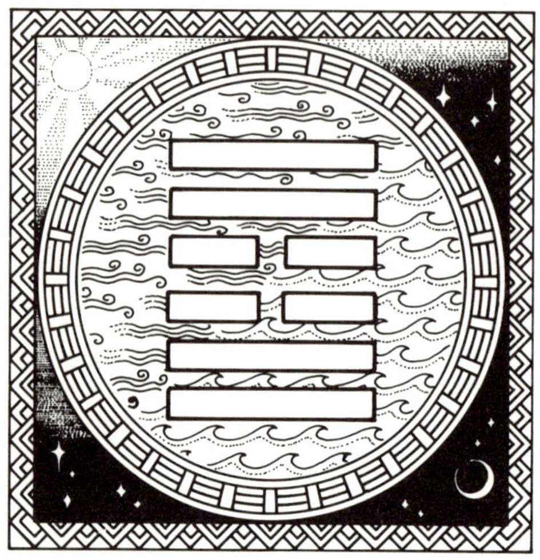

61. CHUNG FU
Influencing Others

Sun over Tui
Wind over Lake

The Image
The unseen power of the wind can move the surface of a lake and thereby show its force. The mind of a wise person seeks to penetrate below the surface of things so that he may understand the actions of others. With such understanding, one will know when to pardon and when to punish with absolute fairness. Others will appreciate such wisdom.

The Judgement
It is easy to persuade those who are receptive to one's ideas but very difficult to convince those with whom one has nothing in common. To influence the latter one must discard preconceived prejudices and find a common ground for approach. Then it will be possible to influence others and achieve great things. It is important to understand that this does not imply compromising one's principles for the sake of the project. True success can only come when one adheres vigorously to what is right.

The Lines
9 in the 1st
To maintain one's inner strength and integrity it is necessary to hold to what is right in one's dealings with the outside world. To seek success by secret agreements with others can only lead to doubts of their sincerity and loss of trust in all things.

9 in the 2nd
If we speak out from the truth in our heart, our words will gain ready recognition from those of like feeling. One's influence does not have to be overtly proclaimed for it will spread out of its own accord. Deliberate attempts would, in fact, inhibit the spread of our ideas. With deeds it is the same. Overt acts arising from inner feelings can have great effects.

6 in the 3rd
If we take our strength from others rather than from our own inner self we can never fully be in charge of our lives. The moods of others control our own – a state which we should consider carefully.

6 in the 4th
To guide us through life it is sensible to pay heed to those who are wiser. This does not mean that we should always be looking to colleagues for guidance, because it is essential to maintain one's own direction. We should be humble in the face of greater knowledge but not allow this to convince us that one person's path is necessarily better than another's.

9 in the 5th
A true leader possesses the strength of personality to unite all his followers in their hearts as well as in their actions. This alone gives the stability needed to overcome difficulties.

9 in the 6th
Words alone are not enough. They must be backed by deeds if success is to be achieved.

62. HSIAO KUO

Attention to Detail

Chen over Ken
Thunder over Mountain

The Image

The sound of thunder resounds more in the mountains than it does in the open. The worthy person is, likewise, apart from ordinary people, who may think his attention to detail unnecessary. Yet the wise person is quiet and humble in his thoroughness, shunning the ostentatious acts of the masses.

The Judgement

The wise person is thorough and modest in all he does. He appreciates the dangers of going beyond his abilities, but works to capacity within them. In this way he achieves success.

The Lines

6 in the 1st

The wise person does not press for changes before all is ready. He is content to work within the system lest premature action brings failure.

6 in the 2nd

There are times when one's duty necessitates taking unusual steps. If the traditional approach is not possible, there is no harm in the restrained use of a new method within the structure of the old organisation.

9 in the 3rd

There are times when it is foolish to neglect the vulnerability of our own position. An overconfident disregard for small precautions may leave one open to avoidable misfortune.

9 in the 4th
Inner resolve must be tempered with the ability to respond to external conditions. It is dangerous to force one's way forward without the assistance of others. Outward inactivity does not imply loss of inner strength.

6 in the 5th
Even a leader of exceptional character cannot achieve success without the assistance of helpers. He is not deluded into thinking that those who are most famous are necessarily the best. He seeks the people who remain modest despite their own great achievements.

6 in the 6th
The wise person acts in accord with the times. When small achievements are sufficient, he does not seek to make great changes, for that would not be in accord with the situation and must therefore result in failure.

63. CHI CHI
Turning Point

K'an over Li
Water over Fire

The Image
Warm water in a pot on the fire is in a perfect state. Too much boiling water will overflow and put out the fire but too little will boil away. The wise person recognises the same problem in the affairs of Mankind. One must be prepared for danger because any change at such a time will produce problems.

The Judgement
When the new order has taken over from the old everything appears to be proceeding smoothly. The wise person at such times is ever mindful of possible problems and diligently works on the small details so that bad practices may not take root.

The Lines

9 in the 1st
When great changes have just occurred the mass of people are pressing forward to create new situations. Many will go beyond the limits of what is sensible. The wise person will slow his actions and thus prevent serious losses.

6 in the 2nd
After a period of change those who have come to positions of authority often neglect to encourage good people. Those of real worth do not seek to push themselves forward. They are content to quietly develop their

own characters, secure in the knowledge that time will bring its just rewards.

9 in the 3rd
It is a natural tendency of all things, be they on the personal, business or government level, to seek to expand their influences, once a firm base has been established. Such expansion often requires great sacrifices and the large organisation which results, constant attention. It is a serious mistake to appoint inferior persons, who are not compatible with success at the centre, to look after more distant projects.

6 in the 4th
When things in general are proceeding well, it is all too easy to gloss over defects and imagine they are trivial. The wise person is always concerned with such apparently minor problems, for he knows that without proper attention more serious consequences will occur.

9 in the 5th
In all matters it is the heart which is of importance and not the outward show. Simplicity coupled with sincerity is always of greater worth than grandiose displays.

6 in the 6th
When one has overcome a problem there is a tendency to boast of one's success. By such attention to the past we may leave ourselves unprepared for the future. Give one's mind to the way forward and thus avoid its pitfalls.

64. WEI CHI
Creating Order

Li over K'an
Fire over Water

The Image
When fire is over water they are not in their natural relationship because the heat of fire rises and therefore is without effect on the water below, which drains downwards. The wise person seeks first to place himself in a position from which he can see things as they really are. Then he is able to place them in a true and proper relationship to one another.

The Judgement
Conditions are always difficult when order is being created from chaos. Success can be achieved if one carefully considers the course of action and is able to convince others to work together for the common cause. It would be a foolish person who at this stage rushed blindly forward.

The Lines

6 in the 1st
When everything is chaotic one feels the need to move forward and start restoring order. To attempt to do this prematurely, however, is to invite failure.

9 in the 2nd
Although the time is not yet ripe for action it is important to prepare oneself inwardly for the advance. One must keep the objective clearly in mind, even though one can take no useful action.

6 in the 3rd
When the time for action arrives we must ensure that we are strong enough to grasp the opportunity. With the help of others, one can achieve success.

9 in the 4th
Now that the time of actual conflict has arrived it is essential to devote all one's energies to the completion of the task. There must be no second thoughts. What is achieved now will provide the basis of future benefits.

6 in the 5th
Success has been achieved and a leader with strength of character has taken command. Able helpers will assist with developments. True success is now seen in vivid contrast to the error of the old ways.

9 in the 6th
Success is a time for rejoicing, but exuberance must not exceed reasonable bounds or that which has been gained will be thrown away by error.

Some Further Reading

Blofeld, J. (1965) *The Book of Change*. London and New York.

Chu, W. K. and Sherrill, W. A. (1980) *The Astrology of the I Ching*. Routledge and Kegan Paul Ltd.

Da Liu (1974) *T'ai Chi Ch'uan and the I Ching*. Routledge and Kegan Paul Ltd.

Foster, D. (1975) *The Intelligent Universe*. Abelard Pub.

Koran, Al (1972) *The Magic of the Mind in Action*. A. Thomas, Pub.

Legge, J. (1964) *I Ching: Book of Changes*. (edited by Ch'u Chai and Winberg Chai). New Hyde Park, New York.

Mulford, P. (1979 – 25th edition) *Thought Forces*. Bell and Hyman Ltd.

Over, R. van (1971) (Edited version of the J. Legge translation) *I Ching*. Mentor Books, The New American Library Inc.

Peale, N. V. (1975) *Positive Thinking for a Time Like This*. Prentice Hall Pub.

Sherrill, W. A. and Chu, W. K. (1977) *An Anthology of I Ching*. Routledge and Kegan Paul Ltd.

Wilhelm R. (1978 reprinted 3rd edition, English translation by C. F. Baynes) *The I Ching or Book of Changes*. Routledge and Kegan Paul Ltd.